Cash Flow for Business Owners

Fast Easy and Reliable Methods to Give You
Residual Income through Investing

Tunita Bailey

Cash Flow for Business Owners
Fast Easy and Reliable Methods to Give You Residual Income through Investing

Written by Tunita Bailey

©2018

Manufactured in the United States of America

For information, please contact:

Ms. Tunita Bailey

The Money Lady

610 Uptown Blvd Suite 2000

Cedar Hill, Texas 75104

info@msbthemoneylady.com

Customer Care 469-844-7577

Website Information

www.msbthemoneylady.com

ISBN 978-1-387-97858-8

DEDICATION

I would like to personally dedicate Cash Flow for Business Owners to all the entrepreneurs that have always known there was a greater calling for your lives. To all that just knew that working a job was great for other people however determined it was just not for you and decided to go against the grain and follow your own route. To those that have gone through hell and high water and finally made it to the shore safely.

To my husband, John, who worked diligently for 29 years at the Fire Department working to support our family, paying all the bills when times were tough and pushing me to follow my dreams and pursue my passions as a business owner and entrepreneur. To my daughters Jasmine and Jade for being understanding and supporting me when I needed it most. To my son Jonathan who focused on his academics and my nephew Anthony Berryman for never giving up.

To my many friends that challenged me, inspired me, prayed for me and encouraged me along the way.

You all have inspired me in ways you could never imagine. Thank you for giving me the gift of having you in my life.

Tunita Bailey

PREFACE

Are you a hopeful entrepreneur who wants to bring your business plan to the world but worries how you'll finance your dream?

Are you a business owner struggling to maintain cash flow for expenditures and payroll? Do you worry how you will stay afloat today, much less finance your ideas for progress tomorrow?

Or are you a successful entrepreneur looking for ways to improve your investment strategies so that you can continue to grow and prosper?

If you've said yes to any of these questions, keep reading ...

Cash Flow for Business Owners provides keen practical information that will guide you through the process of obtaining capital to build a strong personal and business foundation while taking advantage of investment opportunities that create residual income.

You'll discover how to create a millionaire mindset while learning how to access lines of credit of up to $100,000, and how to use it to generate residual income through property investment; the Top 3 Investment strategies for Entrepreneurs; and much more.

LEARN HOW...

- Discover how to become a business owner who invests
- Learn how to access capital for your business
- Discover how and why you should create a corporate entity for investing
- Learn investment strategies that create residual income with residential or commercial real estate.
- Learn the 7 Steps to Creating Residual Income through Investing

TABLE OF CONTENTS

MY JOURNEY

As I sit here on the patio listening to the bird's chirp, I am reminded of my journey over the past year that has pushed me to the point of showing signs of having a stroke. My health was in trouble. It was sudden and unexpected. I had no idea how bad it had gotten, yet I knew it was not good. I was constantly stressed and worried about my business and my financial situation. As it turned out, my blood pressure was 190 over 110 and I began to have headaches in my sleep. When my left side became numb, I knew it was time for a change. I was not going to let myself die unfulfilled at least not today. I knew there had to be more for me. This was not the end. I felt panicked. I thought to myself, *oh my God what are you telling me. What do you want me to do? Where do you want me to go?* I could not imagine leaving this earth without fulfilling my destiny, my purpose or the plan you had for my life. At that point, I knew I was ready to get it done. I get it. It is crystal clear. I am 51 years old and experiencing financial hardships like I have never seen before. In other words, I am broken. I knew I was meant to fly but felt as if my wings had been clipped. I have been trying it my way for a long time and had finally realized that it is God's way or no way. I can get on the highway going the direction you want me to go or I can continue to wonder in my land of wilderness. The wilderness is nowhere to be. At least not for a business owner.

You know you are in the wilderness when you are working harder than ever before, marketing the business 24/7, phones ringing off the hook, and you have a drawer full of clients and yet cannot make ends meet. This was the true wake up call for me. When you must rely on the cash flow from the rental properties or ask your kids to loan you money to pay your bills all while calling yourself 'The Money Lady', something is seriously wrong.

When I finally stopped crying and feeling sorry for myself, I decided to embrace all the personal development information I had been listening to and learning from over the past few months. The daily study of the book Think and Grow Rich and The Laws of Success by Napoleon Hill provided the proven and timeless success principles used to create many millionaires, yet my finances had been unmoved. Here I am again, I thought to myself. I am at the end of another month and it appears I would be singing the same song of brokenness from the previous months.

Pushing forward, I was sitting in yet another 3-day workshop hearing the same basic information and understanding what it takes to obtain financial freedom. At first, I was excited. I felt that maybe this was it. The last workshop that I needed to finally get in the zone to gain the profits my business needs and that I desired.

The Millionaire Mindset Intensive workshop was scheduled to last for the entire weekend from 8 am to 7 pm Friday, Saturday and Sunday and by 3:00 pm on the first day, I made a critical decision. No more workshops or seminars. I was filling my mind and my time with more knowledge. Knowledge is good, but knowledge without inspired action is completely useless. I knew it was time to make a change. It was time for me to take control of my situation and take immediate action. I could not sit idly by and wait any longer. It was time for a seriously massive life change. It was time to stop listening, stop talking and start doing what needed to be done. Successful people take action.

I called my husband and asked him to make reservations at our preferred resort in Tyler, Texas from Sunday to Tuesday. I had to get away. This was it. I knew I needed some time to be alone, so I could just sit, think and work out a plan of execution. I simply wanted to focus on completing all the projects and implement some of the ideas using the success strategies I had learned over the past year. I just needed some time to think and grow rich.

Sunday evening, I cooked dinner as usual for my family after attending church. My daughter Jasmine and her new friend Timothy came to spend the weekend with us. I let everyone know under no circumstances would my plans be altered. This was the time that I would take to figure things out and make an immediate shift in my life. I planned to leave right after dinner to go away and start my new journey.

I packed my bags the night before in anticipation of leaving right after dinner. There was no chance of changing my mind. It was either life or death for me. Literally. This had to happen, and I knew it was my only shot. I could feel it. Shortly after dinner and after saying my goodbyes to my husband, my son and daughter, her new friend and Louie (the best dog in the world), I gathered my bags and put them in the car. By this time, the excitement was building inside me. I was ready. I packed some of the leftovers I had cooked for dinner and I was on my way.

During the drive to the resort, I spent some time thinking about all that I had been through. This confirmed my decision to take this trip for myself and this aroused my thinking more about using my mind and my gifts to infuse my business with something new. The book Think and Grow Rich was in my head again, I knew I would be guided and this is the trip that would help me figure it all out.

In about 1 hour and 45 minutes I was standing at the counter checking in at Silver Leaf resorts in Tyler, Texas requesting a room with a view and telling the lady I would only need 1 key. She asked me twice. *"Are you sure you only need one key?"* she asked. I responded quickly, *"Yes Ma'am!"* I thought about it for a second and thought maybe she thinks I am running away from something because she asked where I drove in from. I told her I had driven from my home in Dallas. I did not elaborate because I felt she was really asking me *'where is your family or friends'*. I guess this is a typical question for a woman alone in a resort lobby not attending a convention or conference, and it felt awfully personal. As I was about to tell her my story when I realized that I do not want to have to tell her what was in my heart. I do not want to have to say I left them at home because I am dying inside and needed the quiet time to save my life. I did not feel the need to disclose that it was this trip that I needed so desperately to spend some time discovering the truth so that I could free myself from this roller coaster of feast or famine life that I had been on for the last 25 years. So instead, I stayed quiet and smiled. I kept the confusion and the anguish all bottled up inside. I wanted to share, but at that time, I knew I needed to just focus on me and that my story would be told when I was ready. So, I quietly waited while she completed the paper work and she gave me the key.

I checked into my room. Put my things away and immediately felt at peace. I decided to go to the store and get a few items, so I would not have to leave the room for any reason while I listened to God and created what I knew was a new and invigorating plan which He would have for my life. I created an agenda for myself. I decided that I would make every moment count. I would not waste any time. Not this time.

On the way down to the resort, I called my assistant to let her know I would not be coming to work until Wednesday and gave her instructions on what needed to be done for the few clients we were working on. Hence the problem; Not having clients of substance was the reality. I had many clients, but none that really brought in a large amount of profits. It has been almost a year and a half since I decided to start this journey of being self-employed all over again. I decided for the last time to burn the ship. I would never ever look for another job. I will be who I am - An entrepreneur - A business owner. I was going to make this work once and for all. I could feel it inside me and I knew this trip was the way to make it work. I would get the answers that I longed for. I would put the wheels in motion once I figured out the plan.

"I" is the magic word in these statements. It was going to be me and I knew I had the power within me and with God beside me to make the changes that needed to be made. I was going to make this work because I had no choice. I was going to do it better than I had ever done it before with my other businesses. I was going to create a mega business with money falling out of the sky. I was going to be able to pay for my household expenses, pay my debts, pay for my kids' college expenses as promised and begin to establish a retirement account and actually save money. I was going to rebuild my real estate portfolio and create cash flow. This was the plan. It is now September 2014 and I am still broken, busted and disgusted. What Is the problem?

Let's take a look...

In January of this year, I started on a journey of personal discovery. I discovered I did not have a millionaire mindset. I had a poor man's mentality. I had been doing the same things expecting different results. Little did I know at that time that this is the definition of insanity and all that I was accomplishing was running myself into the ground. I had been working hard and not thinking hard. That was precisely the problem. I had been starting, stopping, creating, discovering, and changing every day or every week. Every week I was working on something new. I was advising my staff that we would be doing this or that this week. They all knew that Monday's would be the day we implemented a new strategy to make money. After two weeks of working the new plan and payday came around it was apparent that the new strategies had not worked. Again, I had no money for payroll or expenses. I simply could not understand the problem. All of the ideas sounded good. They looked good on paper and the staff was excited when I unraveled the plan for the week. But clearly after a few times of doing this and the results were not changing, something different was in order. Then it hit me. It is not about my plan or putting my plan into action. It is and always will be God's plan. He is the one that makes men successful. But only if we use the gifts and talents that he has given us for the benefit of others. All this time I thought I was supposed to make money for myself and my family and then I realized that this journey is not about me. I had to go through this process to realize that I needed to serve others. This is the key! I needed to create financial freedom for others instead of focusing on my desires, my dreams and my destiny. This is the biggest lesson that I have learned.

I had been listening to the Think and Grow Rich Mastermind calls every day. I began to understand I had to make some major and definite plans. These plans should be expressed daily and massive action must be taken to see fulfillment. I made the plan that I would speak and serve others. I would travel the country and educate the world on how to become financially free using the financing strategies and investment techniques that I have created for others and personally experienced over the last 27 years of my career in the mortgage and real estate industry. I decided I would serve 200 clients over the next 6 months. This filled me with inspiration and a new-found purpose. This was God's plan for my life and I would share with others. It was not just about becoming financially free for my life but about sharing financial freedom with others.

As fate would have it, I was at the gym working out and one of the members mentioned to me that The Small Business Expo would be in town in April of this year. I thought okay, I would like to go and see what other small businesses are doing and maybe I could participate. I immediately got the information and made the call to see what it would take to get a booth at the event. After a few minutes talking to the rep, and quickly discovering that the cost of $10,000 for a vendor booth would not fit into my already negative budget. So, I decided this year I would just attend and maybe in subsequent years I would get a vendor booth and participate on a higher level. It was a small disappointment, but I knew I had to pass for financial reasons. But for now, I would simply listen and learn. I went to multiple vendor booths checking out various information sessions about growing your business. I zeroed in on 2 speakers. One speaker sponsor talked about writing a book and using it as a marketing piece to expand your business. They offered a free weekend workshop to begin to understand how to market yourself as an author and increase your business by becoming an expert or an authority in your field. I signed up for the event paid the $97.00 fee and planned to attend the event.

They saved the best for last. It was Bill Walsh, America's Business Expert. He is a business coach and not the football player to clear up any confusion. He gave a great presentation and afterwards he explained that he was looking for speakers to travel the country and speak. He further explained, you must be expert in your field and have a scalable and product that would convert. He announced after the event he would hold a special session for those that wanted to join his team and speak and sell from the stage. Talk about a plan coming to life! This was exactly what I had decided to do. I would speak and teach individuals how to achieve financial freedom by providing access to capital to fund real estate investments. It was as though God plucked me out of the negative situation and planted me into this place exactly where I needed to be. There is a right place and right time for everything.

I stayed for the speaker's session and out of 200 people, I was selected to be one of the speakers that would attend the speakers training. This meant that I would learn to speak and sell from the stage. I did not know how I was going to pay the $15,000 fee he charged to come to the event, but I had decided that I would not miss this opportunity. No matter what. I signed up for the event and made payment arrangements for the fee and made my flight and hotel arrangements to attend the event in July. I was ecstatic.

It is funny when you decide to do something, and when you have a clear why, the how will take care of itself. The universe seems to make a way for it to happen. God made a way for it to happen. I was put in that place without a vendor booth on purpose. This was my purpose.

I went back to the office and began focusing on making the money I would need to make this new dream of becoming a speaker and serving others a reality. I was able to close several loans just in time to have the funds necessary to start my journey to my new life as a speaker. I knew I was on the right track when I told my husband that I had been selected to join the speakers team and he was excited for me. He even agreed to attend the weekend workshop here in Dallas. He gave me thumbs up after seeing the other candidates speak and checking out Bill Walsh's credibility. This part was just the beginning.

Speakers Journey

The speakers training started on July 25 in Chicago Illinois at the home of Bill Walsh. It lasted for 5 full days. It was an absolutely life changing event. I got a chance to meet some phenomenal people that were on the same path and headed down the same road to becoming successful and professional speakers. I took the valuable information, embraced the millionaire speaker's mindset and turned my intellectual property into a comprehensive product line designed to show business owners how to create Cash Flow.

Turning My Business into a Cash Cow

Once I discovered that serving others ultimately saves you, I began to create systems for my business using my own intellectual property. It worked. I was able to successfully turn my business into a cash cow by using the time-tested real estate investment strategies I have outlined in this book.

If you are looking for fast, easy and reliable methods to create residual income for your family, read on...

One of the first steps of the journey is to build on a solid personal foundation. Let's look at how you should start the process.

BUILDING A SOLID PERSONAL FOUNDATION

I learned early on that when you are working with money and finances, you need a financial advisor. If you do not have one, go out and get one.

This is instrumental in having a solid personal and financial foundation for your business. Having a financial advisor is the key to placing your money in secure hands and in knowing how to create your personal foundation. Then, it is time to sit down with your financial advisor to breakdown your money purpose.

One of the first discussions you should have with your financial advisor is to uncover your personal goals and objectives. Understanding those objectives allows you to quickly establish a roadmap to success.

Once you know where you are you can quickly determine the best route to get to the desired destination. Also, your financial advisor is trained in the specifics of financial management and can best guide you on how to focus and breakdown your financial strategies.

In this chapter we will discuss some of the personal building blocks that are essential in building a solid personal foundation starting with your mindset.

CHAPTER 1
DEVELOPING A MILLIONAIRE MINDSET

Your Financial and Success Mindset Matters

In January 2014, I began my journey to the mastermind mindset. I was sitting in a meeting with other mortgage consultants desperate to make money anyway I could but did not want to continue doing the same thing the same old way. I knew something had to change. I realized that I did not want to continue pursuing the same patterns of behavior that I had been cycling through. In other words, I did not want to continue to be insane. So, as we were ending our meeting about the new mortgage procedures and products, one of the consultants mentioned a daily call designed for entrepreneurs where you learn about the success mindset which is also termed the mastermind mindset. It is designed to empower and build on the entrepreneurs' mindset and enable you to use key principles of proven success strategies to change your life personally and financially.

I immediately wrote down the information and did not hesitate in joining the call the next morning. I quickly discovered that I was not alone in the way I think. There were literally hundreds of entrepreneurs on the line sharing thoughts of how to create a mindset that matters. I felt as though I was not alone in my thought processes. Also, it helped that I was part of a group of people who were all in the same place, advancing their businesses. I realized that it is ok to be extraordinary and different. In fact, it is recommended. This was the place where I needed to be and to be supported by others who were also shifting their mindset.

Although, I had a lot to learn if I wanted to take not only my business to the next level, but I had to go through a complete personal development and mindset change. In other words, I decided to quit being insane and stop doing the same things the same old way and take massive action to create the life I deserve and so desperately desired. Additionally, I was more than ready.

Many people talk about being ready to take massive action and their desire is not backed by action. I was not just ready in my mind, but I was ready to take the desired action necessary to take my business where I wanted it to go. Up. The only way from here was up. I was determined, and I would not be deterred.

I wanted to be a business owner. But I did not want to be just any business owner. I wanted to be a business owner who thrives and is prosperous. I did not want to be a business owner who lives transaction to transaction or waiting on the next deal to close. This is not a way for anyone to live. I wanted to create residual income through my products and services. I wanted to invest in real estate to create the cash flow that would set my family free and allow me to live on purpose. This was my mission and I was going to make it happen.

Every day I thank Felicia Thompson and especially God for opening the door to the Think and Grow Rich Mastermind call where I have begun to reeducate myself on the principles of success. On the call, the leader would read the book for 30 minutes and then would allow the other mastermind members to elaborate on the study of the day. As I listened to the other mastermind members, I decided that I would not only listen, but I would take massive action and began an in-depth study of changing my poor man mentally into a rich man's mindset.

My journey began by listening to the audio cd "Think and Grow Rich" by Napoleon Hill on You Tube. I was simply in awe as I listened to the principles that had literally created millionaires based on understanding the power of how to Think and Grow Rich using the mastermind principles of success.

The first step was to understand what the definition of success means to me and what does it mean to you. Success can mean a lot of things to different people. Success can be money, or it can be accomplishments in business or in one's personal life. Defining success is important because it breaks down how you look at success and then it becomes personal. According to Earl Nightingale's book, The Strangest secret, success is the progressive realization of a worthy idea. It means not conforming and not acting like everyone else. It means doing things differently. It means using your mind to create and develop new things, using your mind to conceive and believe you can achieve and become what you think about. I allowed myself to digest this definition and use it as part of what I believe success to be. Then I worked on my own ideas to develop my business. So, this is what I did. I started thinking and doing things differently.

As I began to embrace the principles of success, I realized that success is not necessarily about making money. It is about being whole. It is about understanding your purpose in life and establishing a plan of action and passionately pursuing it by delivering your personal services in excellence. It is about believing in yourself and your ability to burn the ships as you are crossing the deep waters of life and never looking back. It is about having faith and acting like your vision has come into fruition.

The second step in the journey to changing your mindset is to create a major definite purpose for your life. Write it down, record it and repeat it to yourself every day.

When I made the decision to create my major definite purpose for my life, I immediately began to encounter every temptation to sway my decision. The strong negative vibes began not only from outside sources such as my friends and business associates, but from within my own family. Yes, this happens so be ready for it. You think they will support you and to some extent they do. But, this is part of the change that comes with creating a success mindset. People will try to put you down or tell you it will not work. They will laugh, make fun and joke that this time will be just like the last time.

This is when you need to be the strongest and have your plan in action for when this happens. Fortunately, I was ready for the attacks. I immediately began repeating my major definite purpose and listening to more audios that allowed my mindset to stay on the success path. These audios were the key for me. I also took a ton of notes for reminders and to keep my mind clear of negativity. I carried my mission and purpose with me everywhere. Negativity can come from anywhere and I found that the more prepared I was to deal with it, that I was able to deflect it quickly. Then once I deflected the negative comments and shook it off, I went right back into my success mindset.

The third step is to create a freedom vehicle that you will use to accomplish your major definite purpose. In other words, define how you will accomplish the purpose with a plan and take massive action to accomplish your purpose. A famous quote from Napoleon Hill states: Dreams are the Seedlings of Success. One of the mastermind members added a profound statement that literally drove the point home to me by adding the following:

"Dreams are the seedlings of success, but massive action is the water that makes it grow". In other words, unless you act, you can dream about success as much as you like, but until you act, you will not have success. Then it became clear to me. I had been taking action, but new inspired action was necessary to fulfill my dreams.

As CEO, my major definite purpose is to use my gifts and talents to impact the lives of others by providing financial solutions, education, housing opportunities, and investment strategies to individuals that desire a financial change for themselves and their families. This desire was for me, but it was also for others. This is how I was going to help others to achieve their dreams as well.

My freedom vehicle allows me to offer business owners financing alternatives that allows them to obtain cash for their small businesses. It also allows me to offer residential and commercial lending options for individuals buying real estate. Although I had dreams of being successful in making six figures this year, I quickly realized that If I was going to achieve what my mind had conceived and believed I had to take massive action to assure my purpose would become a reality. So, I started to put the wheels in motion and did just that. I put together an action plan.

I began to look at my business and create systems that would allow me to be more consistent in marketing my personal services.

CHAPTER 1 ACTION STEPS

Reposition Yourself and Create a Success Mindset

In order to create Cash Flow, you must create a success mindset. Therefore, it is important to either listen to the following audio CD's on proven success strategies or read the following books as soon as you can. These texts are: Think and Grow Rich, The Laws of Success, and the 17 Principles of Personal Achievement, by Napoleon Hill, Millionaires Mindset by Brian Tracy, Awaken the Giant Within by Tony Robbins, The Science of Getting Rich by Wallace Wattles and the Strangest Secret by Earl Nightingale. Personally, I listened to the audio CDs, but you can also find them in book format. You can find them in any book store or online. Regardless how you take in the information, these texts will challenge your thought processes and begin to allow you to become more creative and use your imagination to generate new ideas on ways to improve or enhance your existing business. This is the key to changing your mindset and getting to where you want to be. Remember as a man thinketh so shall he become. If you think you can be successful, you can be successful. If you think you cannot be successful, then you will not be successful. It is really that simple and it is all within your mind. Challenge yourself to create a success mindset and with this you have the power to change your life. I did it and so can you.

CHAPTER 2
THE POWER OF THINKING NOT WORKING TO GROW RICH

I had not realized this before but how you think is vital to your success. I never realized the power of thoughts until I became a business owner. I was working so hard yet hardly working. I was not being productive. I was not making full use of the power of my thoughts. I was not thinking to grow rich. I was working and thinking my hard work would make me rich but did not realize that I was a business owner simply working myself to death.

Being a business owner helped me realize how much of an impact my thoughts had on the outcomes for the business. They are the difference in your business success or failure. They are the driving force behind how fast you move in obtaining any of your goals. If you want to change your output, you must first change the input. Once you make the shift everything changes.

Napoleon Hill's Think and Grow Rich is one of the most successful mindset strategy books for entrepreneurs because it teaches principles of success. This book taught me how to strategically go after what I wanted by using the power of my own mind.

With this, you need to know what it is that you want. Then you need to go after this passion or purpose with all that you are and all your being. Once you know what you want, the follow through is reliant upon not only your thoughts but your consistent actions to follow through. However, many entrepreneurs give up too early or have not shifted their mindset effectively then they get stuck or unable to move forward. This makes the difference in being successful and not being successful. The mindset is the biggest part and obtaining new creative ideas and strategies are all part of this mindset. However, it also requires strategic follow through and passion to get things done.

Take time to Think and Grow Rich

Start small and work your way up. Spend at least 30 minutes daily in deep thought. If you cannot do 30 minutes at first, start with 5 or 10 minutes and then work your way up to 30 minutes daily. But be sure to limit your distractions and make this a habit. If you do it, it works. So, make sure that you incorporate this into your daily routine. Every single day. No radio, TV, no computers or no phone or emails. Put yourself in an environment that is completely quiet, so you can be inside your own head. This allows the creativity and thoughts to flow naturally. When you have the distractions of computers, or your phone, TV or radio, you let other things into your thoughts and into your head. Try to let go of your already formulated to do list and find a calm place of peace for 30 minutes. Use this time to generate new ideas not the ones you already have sitting on your plate. Let this be your "letting go" time to any preplanned thinking and really soak in the time that you have. Give yourself this time to think openly and freely. Give yourself this time to Think and Grow Rich.

Then once you have finished these 30 minutes of calm and deep thinking, act and start writing down what your strategies and actions steps will be. Get your pen and paper and make this count. Make a list of massive action steps that you will implement immediately for your business. Take the time to review what you have accomplished thus far and create the plan going forward on exactly how you will achieve more. Do this process daily and you will come up with new ideas and new strategies which you have not thought about previously. This is where the shift in your mindset occurs. Earl Nightingale, who is the author of the book *The Strangest Secret* was a fan of a practice of daily quiet thinking. He encouraged people to do this, so they could come up with new ideas daily for building their business or for creating new ideas that may lead to new business ventures or new possibilities. In fact, this was one of the signature points in his book. Some people call changing your mindset a 'secret' and others call it a strategy. Regardless of the terminology, the most important thing that you can do for your business and for your life is to change your mindset through a daily process of quieting your mind from all the outside noise.

So, taking the time to do this is a crucial step into creating that success mindset. This is because you need this time to dig into your mind and gather all the ideas that have been lying dormant. There are tons of great ideas inside you that will help you make money and fulfill your purpose, but you need to establish a routine distanced from the chaos to do it. Once you do this you'll let newer, fresh and inspirational thoughts in which get your mind generating ideas that you had not previously thought about or even knew existed. You will be amazed at what you can create once you stop and Think and Grow Rich.

Nowadays my favorite strategy is to wake up before the rest of my family. I gather my pen and paper and I make my morning coffee. I go into the kitchen where I know I will not be disturbed, and I sit there quietly. I thank God for my blessings and then I engage in my quiet time. This is where I spend the first thirty minutes in the morning so that I can start the day off right. I consider this to be my time first thing in the morning so that I can gather fresh ideas for my business. Every day I continue to get into the Think and Grow Rich mindset.

The famous motivator and business man Zig Ziglar is famous for saying "People often say that motivation does not last. Well, neither does bathing – that is why we recommend it daily". This is not just for motivation. This is the same for a success mindset. In order to nurture your mindset, you need to condition it daily. Just like people go to the gym or run like they are training for a marathon. This is a process. It is a practice. Thinking and Growing Rich is a daily regimen. I give thanks to God for my path. I sit quietly and evaluate where I am and where I want to go. I evaluate what my business needs. I make a list of the ideas that flow from my mind. I do this in the quiet because from the quiet, the mind is able to generate fresh ideas without interruption. For me, it is a daily decision to get back on the horse and continue to move forward toward success. So, I plan my morning accordingly and I recommend this for others looking to gain a Think and Grow Rich mindset as well. It is a daily practice.

It is not only about thinking differently everyday but conditioning ourselves to reestablish that Think and Grow Rich mindset daily. Engaging in masterminds where others think alike is great too. But allowing yourself at least 30 minutes daily with your thoughts makes a world of difference.

CHAPTER 2 ACTION STEPS

Reposition Yourself with the Power to Think and Grow Rich

The following 10 steps will help you reposition yourself with the power to think and grow rich. Take time to review the action steps and take action.

10 Steps to Reposition Yourself

1. Select a quiet place in your home where you can think
2. Purchase a journal to write down your thoughts
3. Create massive action steps for every idea
4. Record your action steps on your mobile phone and listen throughout the day
5. Create a realistic timeline for successful completion of every idea
6. Create a Think and Grow Rich Calendar
7. Challenge yourself to complete every task
8. Identify an accountability partner or a coach
9. Celebrate your success
10. Repeat the process

CHAPTER 3
HOW TO BUILD A SOLID PERSONAL FOUNDATION

In June 2012, I decided to open my office and begin to originate mortgage loans. I quickly discovered I would have to become a credit specialist and clean up credit before I could originate the mortgage loans. I had to learn the process of restoring and rebuilding credit for my customers prior to securing financing.

Here are some of the specifics regarding personal credit.

Personal Credit

Personal credit has been important throughout history, and it continues to become more important. The world has become a much bigger place, and therefore your credit score is used more often. Because lenders and other service providers cannot possibly know everything about you, they check your credit. Your credit is like a personal history of your behavior with previous creditors. They look at this and evaluate your past behavior to determine whether your future actions. Then, based on what they find this determines whether you will get the loan, job or credit application approved. Also, credit is the primary foundation in which people use to purchase higher ticket items such as cars and homes. Many people either cannot or choose not to pay cash for larger purchases and so the use of personal credit is fundamental being able to complete to the transaction.

Knowing how the credit world works will empower you to manage your credit to your own advantage. You can start to think of your credit as your friend, not a skeleton in your closet. Your credit score can get you things that you want and it can help you save money. You should have a clear idea of what your credit is, and how credit scores function in your life.

Also, if you have a less than stellar credit rating, do not be afraid to find out what it will take to improve your credit score. This is not something to be afraid of or ashamed of. But it is a time to do something about it and take action. Also, if there is something on your credit report that is not yours or seems fraudulent you will want to report it. Taking your credit score seriously and putting your personal credit in order will be vital to getting you where you want to go. It is therefore important that you know about your personal credit and your credit score.

Credit Scores

You can obtain a free copy of your credit report annually. I advise all my clients to obtain a mortgage copy of their report and sign up for a monitoring service to assure your credit profile is being managed. If there are any discrepancies or inaccuracies, these need to be addressed immediately. Remember what gets measured gets managed. Also, staying on top of your personal credit score can help you stay abreast of your current credit situation. This helps you to know your credit standing and will also help you better manage your credit to improve your score if necessary.

Credit Scores determine Positive or Negative Results

Banks, mortgage lenders, credit card companies and other types of lenders use the credit score to evaluate your credit history. They want to know if you are a good risk or a bad credit risk. The credit score is just one factor that they use when deciding if they will give you a loan or not. Also, it is an important factor because it also is used to help determine the interest rate that will charged, the credit limit, and other issues concerned with the loan. Therefore, if you can improve your credit score, this should be done ahead of time, so you can take advantage of a higher credit rating.

The exact formulas for calculating credit scores are closely held secrets, but the Fair Isaac Corporation has revealed that the following components are normally used and given the approximate value:

> ➢ 35 percent punctuality of payment in the past (only includes payments later than 30 days past due).

> ➢ 30 percent the amount of debt, expressed as the ratio of current revolving debt (credit card balances, etc.) to total available revolving credit (credit limits).

> ➢ 15 percent length of credit history.

> ➢ 10 percent types of credit used (installment, revolving, consumer finance).

> ➢ 10 percent recent search for credit and/or amount of credit obtained recently.

Credit scores range from 300-850.

Consider these digits as the two frontiers of your life. For 850 means, you can get a loan to buy an island, a luxury villa, and a yacht. For 300, on the other hand, means that your credit is so bad that your loan is likely to be rejected. A good score for obtaining financing is a range of 620-720. Having a score in this range is highly desirable, so keep this in mind when reviewing your own personal score.

4 Quick Ways to Increase Credit Scores

You can always rebuild your credit if you understand the process. There are 4 quick ways to increase your credit scores and rebuild your credit:

1. **Secured Credit Cards**

    You may want to start with a secured credit card. It requires a deposit as your credit limit. Your credit limit will be raised in the future if you have shown good financial behavior. It is likely that many credit card companies will reject people with bad credit history but utilizing a secured credit card will help you to recover your credit fast. This is highly recommended.

2. **Gas Station Credit Card**

    If you need to buy gas, send your car for service, or buy meals in the gas station, you can consider applying for Gas station credit card. If use it carefully, it can help to rebuild credit history. The available credit might be low at first, but again using this card responsibly will help increase your credit rating and over time the limit will increase.

3. Department Store Credit Card

Department store credit cards can be valuable if used correctly. Since the goods sold in a department store are quite varied, you'll practically be able to buy just about anything you need there. Payment by credit cards is simple but also remember to check your card balance each time you make a purchase. Ensure you do not go over 30% of the total credit line. If your purchases are more than 30% it could appear as though you have a high debt to income ratio. So be sure to charge wisely and pay off monthly to increase your credit worthiness without appearing as though you are in heavy debt.

4. Secured Personal Loan

One of the higher risk options is secured personal loans since it involves your property as collateral to the lender and it normally involves larger amounts of money. Most lenders favor these types of loans since they are secured against your assets. With this type of loan, the bank might ask you to put up your home as collateral or another security may be required by the bank. It will depend on your past credit history, and possible employment status among other things. Either way having this type of loan on your credit with a solid payment history looks stellar on your credit report. It increases your credit worthiness and gives a bump to your overall credit rating.

Personal Unsecured Lines of Credit for Investing

The ability to obtain a personal line of credit can be invaluable if you know how to effectively use it. This can help level up your credit report and increase your credit rating, so you can be trusted with additional lines of credit for investing.

Unsecured credit lines require no collateral, no financials, no appraisals, no tax returns, and no restrictions on use of funds. Qualification is strictly based on the strength of one's personal credit reports and scores. These credit lines can be used to purchase, rehab and flip real estate, allowing a real estate investor to execute more deals and ultimately increase their bottom line on each property.

With an unsecured real estate line of credit, you can draw on and make payments on these credit lines as many times as needed, which means you can flip multiple properties with the same line of credit. This saves you from the transactional cost of working with hard money lenders that make you pay "upfront points."

For real estate investors, it is all about having access to cash to execute deals. The fact is that there are tremendous investment opportunities available in the marketplace right now. So, the people who use these types of loans can leverage their income quickly as they are able to have access to more cash at their fingertips. With real estate credit lines, investors can get the flexibility they need so they can better optimize their real estate investment strategy.

Other benefits of unsecured real estate credit lines include:

- ➢ No upfront fees
- ➢ No reporting to personal credit reports (only reports to business)
- ➢ No documentation
- ➢ No appraisal
- ➢ No collateral
- ➢ No restrictions on use

As every deal is different from one another, real estate investors will find that using various types of financing tools such as unsecured real estate credit lines can provide a great way to finance an investment property. This also allows investors to make more money as they are not tying up their own assets necessarily because they are using the banks money to leverage their own income. For example, an investor gets a loan, invests in a property, flips it and then sells it for more. This allows them to pay off the contractor who improved the property, pay back the original loan, and then pocket the profit from the sale of the flipped property. So, having the ability to use this type of loan is advantageous for the real estate investor and entrepreneur who is looking for more cash flow in their business.

Having access to freely spendable cash without restrictions is what every real estate investor needs in their arsenal whether It is for purchasing investment properties, rehabbing properties, paying off balloon notes, or purchasing raw land; It is clearly a smart choice.

Real Estate Equity Lines of Credit

A Real Estate Equity Line of Credit allows you to borrow against the equity in your own property. The lender will place a lien on the property until the loan is paid in full. You can use your homestead or an investment property as collateral. In most cases you can draw up to 80% of the appraised value of the asset. A major advantage of the equity line of credit is the unlimited availability of the line. If you pay it off each time you can continue using it for investing.

How to Build a Solid Personal Foundation

➤ Take a personal assessment of your personal credit, income and assets.

➤ Create a plan of Improvement for any area where there is a deficit.

➤ Track and monitor your personal financial status monthly.

➤ Secure an unsecured or secured line of credit

Building a solid personal foundation will prepare you for a strong and solid business.

CHAPTER 3 ACTION STEPS

Reposition yourself and build a solid personal foundation

Repositioning yourself personally is a vital step in creating a solid personal foundation. Follow these simple steps to begin the process:

- ➤ Take a personal assessment of your personal credit, income and assets.
- ➤ Create a plan of Improvement for any area where there is a deficit.
- ➤ Track and monitor your personal financial status monthly.
- ➤ Secure an unsecured or secured line of credit

Building a solid personal foundation will prepare you for a strong and solid business foundation. In the next chapter I will explain how begin the process.

CREATING A SOLID
BUSINESS ENTERPRISE

CHAPTER 4
THE ESSENTIALS OF A SOLID BUSINESS

As an entrepreneur, did you know you have a unique opportunity to build, maintain and acquire credit both individually and as a business owner? That's good news if you're trying to build and grow a company because you will not have to rely solely on your personal credit to do that.

Let's look at the differences in using personal credit vs business credit.

Personal Credit Vs Business Credit

At the point an individual with a social security number accepts their first job or applies for their first credit card, a credit profile is started with the personal credit reporting agencies. This profile, otherwise known as a credit report, is added to every credit inquiry, credit application submitted, change of address and job change. The information is typically reported to the credit bureaus by those who are issuing credit. Eventually, the credit report becomes a statement of an individual's ability to pay back a debt.

When a business issues another business credit, it is referred to as trade credit. Trade, or business, credit is the single largest source of lending in the world.

Information about trade credit transactions is gathered by the business credit bureaus to create your business credit report using your business name, address and federal tax identification number (FIN), also known as an employer identification number (EIN), which you get from the IRS. The business credit bureaus use this compiled data to generate a report about your company's business credit transactions. In many cases, those issuing credit to you will rely on your business credit report to determine if they want to grant you credit and how much credit they'll give.

Building your business credit depends on the size of your business among other things. If you are new business, you may be considered a higher risk if you do not have any trade experiences or past credit utilization. It will be important to improve your trade experience and credit utilization over time but also to ensure that your payment habits are good and that you do not have any outstanding unpaid balances. They will also look at your trends over time and your business credit will become public record. Also, when establishing business credit your business will have demographics which include your business classification and business size.

Business credit is good to have and important to have because it can help you when investing. Therefore, it is good to establish good business credit through good credit habits. Pay your bills on time and reduce any outstanding balances as soon as possible that are not regular mortgage payments.

Essentials of a Solid Business

A solid business starts with a solid plan for success. In most cases it begins in the mind of the business owner or entrepreneur. Therefore, it is essential to have a Think and Grow Rich mindset, and a positive success focused mindset. Your plan is not just about your business but also about you, so it should be built with a solid foundation and with a solid plan.

I have listed below the steps in establishing a solid business entity.

1. Form a corporation or LLC to operate your business under and obtain an FIN or EIN from the IRS. You can apply for an EIN number at the IRS website.

I'm suggesting you form a corporation or LLC as opposed to structuring your business as a sole proprietorship or partnership because with a sole proprietorship or partnership, your personal credit information could be included on your business credit report--and vice-versa. In addition, as a sole proprietor or partner in a partnership, you're personally liable for the debts of the business and all your personal assets are at risk in the event of litigation. So, to remove your personal assets and to reduce risk establish an LLC or corporation.

Furthermore, Corporations and LLCs, on the other hand, afford business owners liability protection, and you can build a business credit profile that's separate from your personal assets and debts. You may be able to apply for credit under your business's name and obtain credit without a personal credit check or guarantee if the credit grantor will do so--and It has been my experience that often all you have to do is ask.

2. Register your company with the business credit bureaus

To register a company with the business credit bureaus, Dun & Bradstreet, HSBC Business Credit USA, Experian and Equifax, go directly to the websites of Experian Business, Business Credit USA and Equifax Business and register your business' DUNS and/or Employer Identification Number with each agency. Include your business' legal name and corporate address in the registration application.

3. Comply with the business credit market requirements.

It is extremely important for businesses to meet all the requirements of the credit market to ensure a higher likelihood of credit approval. In fact, not being in compliance with the credit market can raise red flags with both credit bureaus and grantors. The red flags include such simple things as not having a business license or a phone line. Most businesses will not grant credit to another business that hasn't taken the steps to set the company up with the proper licenses and local, state and federal requirements. So be sure to check with your state and local area to become aware of the necessary requirements before filing for credit.

4. Prepare financial statements and create or obtain professional business plan.

These documents are often required by many credit grantors. You can look up business plans online and find a template that you can fill in with your own business goals or business model. Additionally, you can work with your financial advisor to produce one although this may be costlier if you are paying for your advisor's time.

5. Find companies willing to grant credit to your business without a personal credit check or guarantee.

When a company grants your business credit, be certain they report the payment experiences you have with them to the business credit bureau to help build your business credit report and a financial foundation for your company. This will be good for establishing the business credit of your company and for establishing credibility with your business in general. As you build your business credit you will have more leverage with investing because you will have greater access to business loans and will not have to access your own personal funding.

CHAPTER 4 ACTION STEPS

Reposition Yourself to Establish a Solid Business

Reposition yourself with a solid business by reviewing where you are currently. If you are just getting started in establishing your business, follow the steps I have outlined in this chapter.

If you are an existing business take time to pull your business credit report. Take note of your current business ratings. If they are in good standing great job! If not take steps to reestablish yourself as a solid business.

CHAPTER 5
MOVING TO THE FOURTH QUADRANT-BUSINESS OWNER TO INVESTOR

One evening feeling frustrated about ending the week once again in the negative, I contacted one of my friends who is a seasoned business owner and entrepreneur wanting to vent about all the problems I was having with my sales team and overall office production. As we talked, and I told her about each problem and she would offer various solutions. After each solution, I would again hit her with another problem. Then she said asked the magic question are you a business owner who invests? I thought oh my God that's it. I would not be having these problems and feeling so frustrated if I began to concentrate on my real estate investing business. Once I began to focus my energy on creating residential income and building my own solid foundation, having a non-productive week in the office would become a moot point. I immediately went home and began to think about ways to increase my real estate investment portfolio which would create residual income and I would once again become a business owner who invest.

I started the process by listening again to the audio cd by Robert Kiyosaki's Cash Flow Quadrant.

I listened as he explained the 4 Cash Flow Quadrants. They are Employee, Self Employed, Big Business Owner and Investor.

- ➢ Employee (E) – Otherwise known as a job
- ➢ Self-Employed (S) – Small business owners or self-employed (Doctors, and lawyers)
- ➢ Business Owner (B) – Big businesses (500 and more employees). Businesses that are selling products and predefined services.
- ➢ Investor (I) – People like Warren Buffett

Where you are in the quadrant determines whether you will have active or passive income. The objective is to move from employee, self-employed, or business owner to investor.

Here are each one of the Cash Flow Quadrants explained in detail:

E – Employee

Most individuals live in this area. You work for a company and trade your time for money. You go into work, you put in your time and then you go home. This is a money exchanged for time. If you want to earn more money, you must work more hours. Another option for making more money is to go work for another company that pays better or to find a position with a greater salary, or hourly wage. With this position in the quadrant there is no passive income. It is merely an exchange of time for money and there are no bonuses. If you do not work, you do not make any money.

S – Self Employed

This is one step better than an employee, but in reality, you still are trading time for money. You own your own business, but in reality, the business owns you. All your time goes into the business and while you may earn a bigger paycheck you are still responsible for the day to day business but are not necessarily able to leverage additional income. The positive benefit is you have more personal and financial freedom than an employee.

B – Business Owner

A business implies you have a system in place. You have others working for you as employees. You aren't selling your time for money, but rather selling a product or service. In other words, you do not have to be working for the business to generate income. In this model people work for you and while you are employing others, they cost money and you pay them for their time. So, while you are making more money and have more freedom, you also have money tied up in your employees to do the work, so you do not have to. This is a great way to monetize your business but does not create a larger cash flow in which your money creates more money.

I – Investor

This is where you truly have passive income. Your money is making more money, and essentially multiplying while you sleep. Investments like stocks, bonds, and real estate generate an annual cash flow. These are the investments that will allow you to retire. Things you build once and have a long (5-10 year+) timespan in payouts. Additionally, these generate residual income that you continue to earn and grow without your added time. Plus, once you initially invest your money grows with that investment.

To move to the fourth quadrant to become a business owner who invests, I recommend beginning a viable real estate investing business. Before you begin the process, there are some fundamentals about investing you should know. Let's start with the importance of why you should invest in real estate.

Why Invest in Real Estate?

Owing real estate can make a tremendous difference in generating cash flow for most business owners. The type of real estate owned simply determines how much return and how often you will receive cash flow on your investments. Most people start with residential investing.

I have listed several reasons why investing in real estate is crucial in the success of your business:

> ➢ Real estate provides more predictable returns than stocks and bonds.

> ➢ Real estate provides an inflation hedge because rental rates and investment cash flows usually rise by at least as much as the inflation rate.

> ➢ Real estate provides an excellent place for capital in times when investors are unsure of prospects in the stock and bond markets or when investors expect long-term returns in stocks and bonds to be inadequate.

> ➢ The equity created in a real estate investment provides an excellent base for financing other

investment opportunities. Instead of borrowing to get the capital to go into other vehicles (i.e., buying stocks on margin), investors can borrow against their equity to finance other projects. The relative ease in borrowing against a real estate investment combined with the deductibility of the mortgage interest makes this option a less-expensive method for financing other opportunities for investors who are comfortable taking on the additional financial risk.

➢ In addition to providing cash flow for owners during periods when residential real estate is being rented out, it can also be used as a residence or for some other purpose during periods when it is not producing cash flows.

For business owners I think the most important reason to invest in real estate is to create cash flow. The idea is to create enough income to offset unexpected office expenses as well provide a source of revenue to purchase more supplies, equipment or inventory. Investing in real estate creates options.

Business Owner and Investor Sells Properties to Cure IRS Debts

One of my clients owns several investment properties that are free and clear. Recently he contacted me to assist with selling some of the investment properties to pay off some IRS payroll taxes. I immediately began the process of assisting him in marketing the properties and sold 3 properties for cash to low to moderate income borrowers. The net proceeds from those properties were in access of $70,000 in less than 30 days. He was able to successfully fulfill his tax liability along with providing a homeownership opportunity for individuals in need of an affordable home.

As a business owner who invests you could not only provide cash solutions for your business, you are able to provide homeownership solutions for families. A business owner who is in position to serve others creates a win-win for everyone.

CHAPTER 5 ACTION STEPS

Reposition Yourself to Move to the Fourth Quadrant

If you are a business owner and experiencing cash flow shortfalls, first look at which quadrant you are operating in and begin steps to assure you are a business owner who invests.

Here is a practical idea to create additional cash flow for your business.

Properties or Products Create Cash Flow

Most small business owners start in business by leasing space from a landlord. If your business is located near a vacant lot check for special permits that will allow you to create a Parking lot and charge fees. This will allow you to create residual income to use to purchase the building, offset your lease payments or Invest in your own space.

If the parking lot is not an option, create your own product. The idea is to create ways to offset your expenses and create other streams of income that can be converted into additional CASHFLOW that can be used to invest in a long-term income strategy such as real estate.

CHAPTER 6
GETTING TO THE MONEY
FINANCING REAL ESTATE

Financing is my favorite subject. That's why they call me The Money Lady! The ability to offer financing options on all types of real estate allows me the opportunity to be creative when it comes to offering financing solutions for anyone looking to invest in real estate. The options are limitless if you are an owner occupant or an investor looking for funding.

There are programs available that can be tailor made to fit every scenario. I think it is essential to have a general understanding of the options that are available if you decide to purchase residential or commercial real estate or you need cash out of an existing property.

Let's take a look at some of the loan programs that are available to finance any residential or commercial property.

Non-Profit Secures a No Doc Loan for $100,000

One of my clients called me to assist him in selling some of his investment properties for cash. He was attempting to purchase some lots to begin the process of building some new homes. His goal was to sell the properties and pay cash for the lots. Once he gained possession of the lots, he wanted to get funds from the City of Dallas and another non-profit organization to subsidize building the homes. His idea was a good one but was not the most effective way to obtain $100,000 in cash.

Immediately, I informed him about a new program for a line of credit secured by real estate. This program allowed him to access $100,000 in cash secured by real estate with no credit, no income, no appraisal, and no property seasoning.

Specialty Loans No Income, No Credit, No Assets-The No Doc Loan

The No doc loans are back. These loans are based solely on the property. Typically, the property will be free and clear and, in some cases, taxes are generally owed on the property. The No Doc loan will pay off taxes in addition to give the borrower some additional cash for repairs. These loans are designed for residential, commercial properties as well as land.

They are considered no doc loans because there are no financials required. No income, No Assets, No Credit and No appraisal. These loans are the easiest loans to get if you already own the property. The interest rates for these loans are typically interest only loans at 12-14% with a 24-month repayment term.

It is a great program for business owners who already own property and would like to take cash out and invest into a bigger project.

There are other programs offered to business owners that do not already own a home. If you are looking to purchase a home, there are products available for owner occupants with income fully documented or stated income. Let's look at some of the programs for residential loans.

Residential Loans for Owner Occupants Stated and Full Doc

A residential mortgage loan is an extension of credit secured by residential real property. Typically, a single-family dwelling or multiple-family dwelling of four or less units are considered as residential property.

Owner occupant loans are generally considered to be lower risk loans. They offer lower rates and higher loan to values. There are two major types of loans government and conventional loans. Generally, the underwriting guidelines are more liberal to owner occupants due to the expectancy of repayment from the borrowers. The rational is a borrower will pay for a primary residence for his or her family a place to live.

Full Doc Loans

A loan is fully documented if the borrower can provide evidence of the ability to repay the debt. This would include a good credit profile, verifiable income, and verifiable assets. A fully documented file would include tri merged credit report, paystubs, tax returns, bank statements and two forms of identification.

I often would refer to a full doc loan as the 2-2-2. This represented 2 pay-stubs covering 30 days of income, 2 years of tax returns to include company issued W-2's and 2 months of bank statements showing funds to close the loan. When the owner occupant provides the required documentation, they will receive a lower rate and a low-down payment. If the owner occupant or wage earner could not produce the documents required for a fully documented loan, they are given the opportunity to use a stated income program if they have the credit profile that aligns with the stated income program guidelines.

Business owners often do not have what I referred to as a fully documented loan with the 2-2-2 document requirements. If you are self-employed you are required to provide your tax returns for the last 2 years along with a year to date P&L statement. This will sometimes cause a problem for business owners in getting financed because they typically write off all their income to avoid paying taxes. This strategy often will not allow a business owner to qualify for the traditional financing program. In most cases, if they have a strong personal credit profile, they will be offered a stated income program.

Stated Loans

Stated Income Loans were introduced to the lending community to provide lending opportunities to individuals that did not receive income in the traditional way.

These loans offered minimized income documentation but often would have a higher interest rate or larger down payment. These underwriting requirements were used to reduce the risk of default of the mortgage. Residential stated income loan programs are available for both self-employed and wage earners.

A wage earner or employee might use a stated earnings program where the earnings specified on the loan application will not be verified by the lender. This option is only used if the employee receives his payroll in cash or is paid as a contractor.

All self-employed borrowers must provide proof evidence of self-employment. Generally, a letter from their Certified Public Accountant will suffice.

Whether you are self-employed or are a wage earner, excellent credit (680 credit score or higher) is required to qualify for a stated income loan. There are other programs for borrowers with lower credit scores but to get the best rates, a credit score of 720 or higher is preferred.

The requirements for obtaining financing for investment properties as a business owner will often have different qualifications and guidelines. Let's look at the requirements to become a business owner who invests.

First time investors generally begin investing in residential investment properties due to the ease of obtaining financing. Residential investing offers three basic funding programs for financing investment properties. They are residential stated income or fully documented traditional loans. A general understanding of each program will allow you to make an informed decision as you seek financing alternatives for your first investment.

Residential Investor Loans Stated and Full Doc

Residential investor loans are designed for properties that provide housing for individuals or families and contain four units or less on the property.

Typically, residential investment loans will extend for up to thirty years and the rate is generally higher than owner occupant loans, usually between .5% and 1%.

Residential investor loans are available as a stated income program or fully documented loans. The loans require a minimum of 20-25% down. In most cases business owners prefer to go stated and make a larger down payment to avoid providing the income documents that are required for a fully documented loan. The down payment will generally be 20-25% down for both loans however the stated loan is quoted at a higher interest than the fully documented loan. The exit strategy for the property will ultimately determine which program would be best.

Traditional Loans

Traditional financing is available for purchasing investment properties. At the time of this writing new options for investors have emerged. An investor can get up to 80% Loan to Value with low rates. Check with your local mortgage banker or broker for the updated guidelines on traditional funding for investors.

Traditional Loans Vs Hard Money Loans

To streamline the entire process most of my client start their investing business using hard money or private money loans. These loans are easier to obtain, and the property condition requirements are less stringent than traditional financing. Although the rates are higher, and the terms are shorter, business owners who invest often chose the hard money financing route. Let's look at the guidelines for hard money loans and some of the advantages of using these programs.

Hard Money

Hard Money Loans (also called **High Yield Loans**) are generally short-term loans (1-3 years). These loans carry higher interest rates than typical permanent loans, and cost more up-front points to the lenders. In addition, they may have a "back end" fee to the lender when the loan is paid off. These loans are *not* meant to be the final financing solution to a borrower's needs.

The key issue for all Hard Money lenders is "How am I going to get repaid?" If a borrower can reasonably answer this question, he would have a chance at obtaining a Hard Money Loan.

Hard Money loans are ideal for investors who find themselves in any of the following situations:

The investor needs quick financing to take advantage of an investment opportunity, and do not have the time to pursue traditional financing.

The investor has poor credit, and traditional financing sources are shying away.

There are environmental problems at the site, and again traditional financing sources are not interested until the property is cleaned up.

The property they are either buying or already own is not stabilized (possibly has high vacancies that should be fixed soon or does not have enough of a track record to attract permanent financing) and need cash to bring the property to the point where it can qualify for permanent financing.

In each of the above situations, a Hard Money loan would enable the borrower to have the capital to remedy the situation, which would then enable the property to obtain more permanent financing.

Let's talk about some of the advantages of Hard Money Lending.

Advantages of Hard Money Lending

- ➤ Hard Money Loans / No Hassle Financing for Investment Properties
- ➤ Investor Hard Money Financing up to 100% plus rehab costs
- ➤ Close in 7-10 Days
- ➤ No Mortgage Payments
- ➤ No Financial Documents
- ➤ No Credit or Debt Requirements
- ➤ No Down Payment Requirements
- ➤ No Pre-payment Penalty
- ➤ No Cross Collateral needed / New LLC's OK !
- ➤ Finance Multiple Properties
- ➤ Purchases, Flips, Rehabs, New Construction, Const
- ➤ Bail-outs
- ➤ Fast Approvals / Direct Lender!!!
- ➤ Financing up to 75% ARV (after-rehab-value)

REQUIREMENTS:

1) Copy of sales contract + subject property info + pics
2) Itemized list of repairs w/costs
3) Projected sales price
4) 3-comps (MLS comparable)

This hassle-free type of financing for investment properties allows anyone to take advantage of investing in real estate without the hassle of meeting traditional requirements.

I work with several investors who prefer to use hard money simply because of the ease of the transaction. Most of them could get traditional funding but chose to take this route to get in and out of a project quickly.

Whether using traditional or nontraditional financing residential investing is a great place to start for a new business owner looking to get into the game of investing. However commercial investing should also be seriously considered. Often it is not the first choice of beginning investors due to the perceived barriers to entry.

The barriers of entry often include the requirement of a larger down payment usually up to 30% of the sales price and higher fees required upfront for the phase 1 due diligence process which often includes an appraisal and inspections fees up to 1% of the sales price. A business owner could spend up to $2500-$5,000 upfront prior to obtaining final approval for the financing.

Financing for commercial loans are now available as a stated income loan as well as fully documented loans. If you are just starting out as a business owner and have access to the capital required for the down payment and due diligence process, commercial is a great place to start investing.

Let's look at the requirements for a commercial stated income loan.

Commercial Loans-Stated Income

Stated Income commercial financing for investor commercial properties are now available without the requirement of personal or business tax returns. Borrowers are not required to sign a 4506-T (authorization to request tax returns from the IRS), and personal income and personal debt-to-income (DI ratio) are not verified/calculated. This is a huge change in the lending industry for commercial loans. Typically, hard money lenders are the only lenders that offer this program. Traditional banks will require a fully documented loan to assure the borrower can repay the debt. Nontraditional lenders or hard money lenders rely strictly on the income of the property and will often provide a lower loan to value at 65%-75%.

For business owners looking to get into new construction investing, financing is available for building spec homes. Let's look at the requirements.

Construction Loans- Financing Spec Homes

Construction loans for new-built homes are either obtained by the homebuilder or prospective owner. In pre-recession days, small builders had greater access to capital but now must frequently put the onus on the buyer to obtain the loan.

Most new homes rising today are simply "specs" built by big, high-credit corporate conglomerates. However, business owners looking to invest in new construction have the option to purchase lots and hire a builder to build spec homes on those lots to be sold to individuals or to be retained as rentals.

If you would like to become a business owner investing in new construction there are a few basic construction processes, you should become familiar with prior to beginning the process.

Let's look at the basics of a construction loan.

The basics of construction loans

Let's proceed on the assumption that you're taking out an individual construction loan. Such loans, which can be tough to get without a previous banking history because of the lack of collateral (a finished home), have special guidelines and include monitoring to ensure timely completion so your repayment can begin promptly.

Construction loans are typically short term with a maximum of one year and have variable rates that move up and down with the prime rate. The rates on this type of loan are higher than rates on permanent mortgage loans. To gain approval, the lender will need to see a construction timetable, detailed plans and a realistic budget, sometimes called the "story" behind the loan.

Once approved, the borrower will be put on a bank-draft, or draw, schedule that follows the project's construction stages and will typically be expected to make only interest payments during construction. As funds are requested, the lender will usually send someone to check on the job's progress.

Construction-to-permanent arrangement

Upon completion, which is defined by a certificate-of-occupancy issuance and full payment of contractors (and often their signatures on lien releases), the borrower's loan liability will typically roll over into a mortgage, ideally in an arrangement where the borrower pays closing costs only once. Of late, lenders have been combining the two into a single 30-year loan with one closing, called construction-to-permanent financing. Because of the bank's greater loan-to-value risks in these, most buyers are required to put a little more skin in the game.

New Builder in Houston Secures $800,000 Loan for New Condos

Most new builders have a difficult time obtaining financing for new construction. One of my clients in Houston, Texas was able to secure a new loan for $800,000 for construction of 3 new condo units. Although the builder had an A+ credit rating and a complete construction package, he was unable to secure traditional financing. His lack of experience would have prohibited him from obtaining the loan until we were able to identify a viable solution. We were able to partner the new builder with an existing builder who had just completed a similar project. Once the connection was made the project was approved and the new builder was able to secure the necessary funds required to begin construction. The properties were completed in 9 months' vs 12 months and were sold prior to completion. The builders estimated net profit was over $275,000.

Business owners who invest in new construction could potentially make huge profits building new properties. If you are considering this approach as an investment strategy, make sure you have a team of professionals working with you to obtain the funding and a strategic partnership that will assure your success.

CHAPTER 6 ACTION STEPS

Reposition Yourself and Get to the Money

There several ways to *Get to the Money* with real estate. Business owners who make the decision to invest by taking cash out of existing properties or purchasing lots and building new properties can create huge profits.

Here are some practical ways to Get to the Money:

> Purchase lower priced properties for cash and rehab if necessary
> Secure a tenant and Lease the property
> Secured a loan against the property for cash
> Take the cash and purchase lots and build new residential construction
> Secure a Team of Professionals to assist you with each phase of the project
> Pre-Sale the homes prior to beginning the construction process
> Successfully complete the project within the specified time frame
> Close, Fund and Repeat the Process

CREATING RESIDUAL INCOME THROUGH INVESTMENTS IN

REAL ESTATE

CHAPTER 7
HOW TO DETERMINE THE BEST REAL ESTATE INVESTMENT STRATEGY IN 3 EASY STEPS

Successful real estate investors can make money in any economy, in any market, but today's real estate market can make it difficult if you do not know where to start or how to determine which strategy is best for you. Therefore, it is necessary to create an investment strategy plan that lines up with your business goals.

There are 3 factors that determine where you will start on your real estate investment journey. These factors are: Assets, Credit and Income.

Assets- If you have access to capital for investing you can use it to personally buy real estate or allow a partner to use it to invest in real estate. However, when using your own assets, you tie them up in the property which is why so many people rely on credit. Using assets is a great way to advance your business, but if you do not have to rely on assets, there are other options.

Credit- If you have good credit you have the option of getting a personal loan to purchase real estate. If you have challenged credit, your options will be limited. Therefore, it is important to evaluate your credit worthiness and fix any negative credit issues so that you can advance your credit status. Using your credit is a great option in purchasing or investing in real estate for your business.

Income-If you have a verifiable source of income i.e. paystubs and w-2's, and tax returns you are more likely to be approved for a mortgage loan. If you do not have verifiable income, your options are limited to larger down payments and higher interest rates. So be sure to save these documents and keep them in a safe place so that you can access them easily. When you have a verifiable income, you have an advantage.

Here are 3 real estate investment strategies you can implement right now without using any of your own money or credit or income.

1. Quick Flipping – Wholesaling

This is the classic buy low/sell low strategy and it is the best way to make fast cash.

Basically, here's how it works. You find a seller who is motivated. Then you negotiate a low purchase price, and you both sign a purchase contract. Now you can "assign" your contract to another buyer.

For example, you contract to buy a house worth $140,000 for $100,000. You "assign" your contract to your new buyer for $15,000. You never actually "owned" the house, you never used your own money, and your credit was never an issue.

2. "Subject To" the Existing Mortgage

With this strategy, you use the seller's existing financing, taking title "subject to the existing financing." You agree to make the seller's mortgage payments, and the seller gives you the deed. You are now the owner of the property and essentially take over the mortgage.

3. "Soft" Private Money or "Hard" Private Money

The last real estate strategy is the use of hard or soft private money to purchase investment properties. These loans are based solely on the collateral and not based on credit or income. Hard Money is usually much more expensive than other private money.

The maximum loan amount is 65% of market value, the interest rate is very high (usually 14% or higher), and you must pay 4 to 10 "points" for the loan. Each "point" equals 1% of the loan amount.

"Soft" Private Money is usually a lot less expensive than hard money, though it may be tougher to find. Usually they are loans from private individuals. They could be a friend, family member, business associate, or maybe just a professional referral. In any case, their role as a provider of funding is strictly as you agree upon with them which makes it easier to invest without credit, income or assets becoming an issue.

How to Determine the Best Real Estate Investment Strategy in 3 Easy Steps

There are 3 types of investment strategies depending on which category you fall into. They are Investor A, B, or C. Let's discuss each category:

The following chart will allow you to determine what type of investor you are.

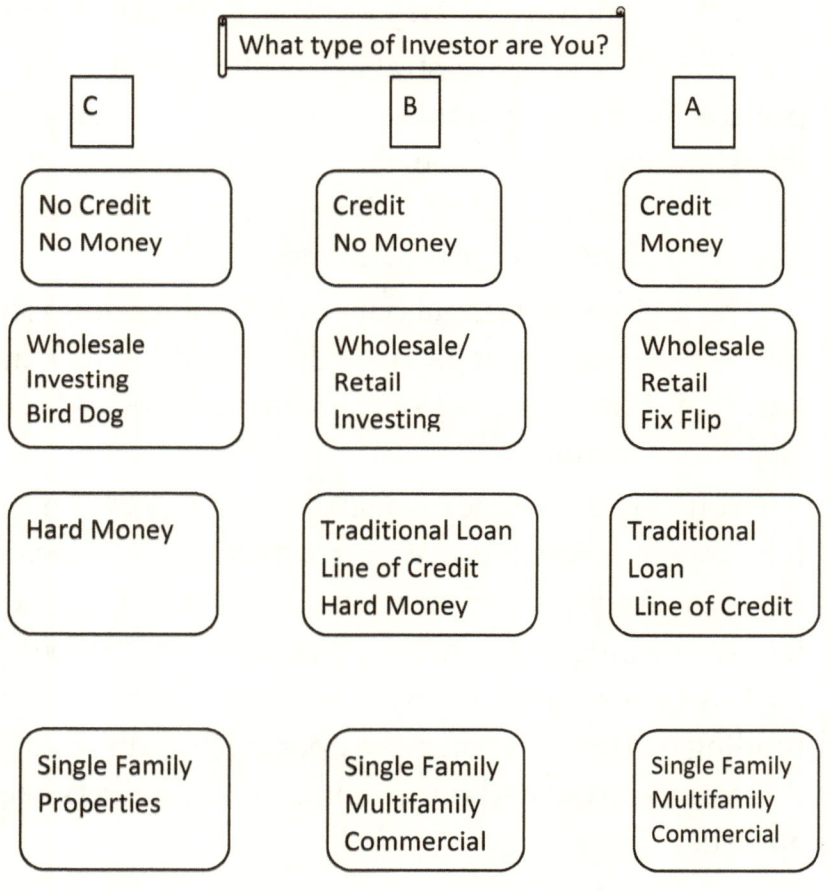

What type of Investor are You?

C	B	A
No Credit No Money	Credit No Money	Credit Money
Wholesale Investing Bird Dog	Wholesale/ Retail Investing	Wholesale Retail Fix Flip
Hard Money	Traditional Loan Line of Credit Hard Money	Traditional Loan Line of Credit
Single Family Properties	Single Family Multifamily Commercial	Single Family Multifamily Commercial

C Investor- No Credit and No Money

If you have no credit and no money, the best option is to wholesale properties or Birddog for other investors until you reach your financial goals. Generally, single-family housing is the quickest way to get access to capital.

B Investor- Credit and No Money

If you have good credit you can obtain loans or lines of credit to purchase any type of investment property.

A Investor- Credit and Money

If you have access to capital and your credit is good the sky is the limit. You can participant in all the investing options, financing options as well as purchase any type of property.

Take a few minutes and complete the following exercise. It will help you determine where you are currently.

Once you determine where you are, you can quickly create a strategy that best fits your personal financial situation and devise a plan that will help you get to the next level of your real estate investing business.

Exercise

Answer the following questions:

1. How is my credit?
   a. Good Credit
   b. Bad Credit

2. Do I want to invest in residential or commercial properties?
   a. Residential
   b. Commercial

3. How will I will fund my transactions based on my current financial situation?
   a. Traditional
   b. Hard money loans

4. How will I get the funds for investing?
   ➢ Wholesaling
   ➢ Line of Credit
   ➢ Borrow from friends or family

5. Based on your review of the chart, what type of an investor are you?
   a. A
   b. B
   c. C

5 Steps to Determine Investment Strategy

I have listed 5 Steps that will help you determine which program is the best investment strategy for your personal situation.

Look at the steps and begin to analyze where you are and what you need to do to change your financial picture.

- ➢ Step 1 Determine your personal financial strength
- ➢ Step 2 Determine which type of property will be your primary focus
- ➢ Step 3 Determine the funding strategy
- ➢ Step 4 Determine exit strategy
- ➢ Step 5 Establish or reestablish your personal finances

Now take some action...

CHAPTER 7 ACTION STEPS

Reposition Yourself

Action #1

Review the chart and determine which type of investor you are based on your current financial situation.

Action # 2

Write down the plan of action to begin your journey to changing your existing situation

Action #3

If you have determined you are ready to begin your investing journey, take the next step within the next 30 days.

CHAPTER 8
WHOLESALING, FIX AND FLIPPING
OR BUY AND HOLDING PROPERTIES

Earlier this year I decided to add wholesaling real estate into my streams of income along with doing loans. I contacted one of my real estate agents that I work closely with and informed her I was looking for a property to purchase. As soon as she located one, she called and said I have a great property in Duncanville that you can purchase. It is a 5-bedroom house, 3 baths and a 2-car garage with a pool. Hot dog! I immediately went to look at the property and discovered it needed about $15,000 worth of work to bring it up to standards. The owner was deceased, and the property had to be sold by order of the courts. One of the owners five children were living in the house and was being ordered to sell the house and split the proceeds to settle the estate. (Hint: they had to sell)

I initially offered $195,000 for a property with an ARV of $350,000. After my contractor reviewed the property and submitted a detail bid for repairs, I discovered the repairs were going to cost much more than I had initially anticipated. I contacted the agent and submitted a copy of the repair list and requested a price reduction based on the increased number of repairs needed to bring the property up to standards. The agent called back and informed me after careful consideration, the owners daughter agreed to the price reduction.

She had already found another place to live and she did not want to lose the house, so she lowered the price. At that point I recognized I had a deal. The house was worth $350,000 and I had it under contract for $185,000. The contracts were submitted to the title company and we were preparing to close the file when the escrow officer called and informed us there were some title issues that would have to be cleared prior to closing the file. She could not give a definite time as to when the file would be ready to close.

While we were waiting for clear title, I got an opportunity to go to a speak and write and make millions conference with Lisa Nichols in Newport Beach California for 10 days. This was an opportunity of a lifetime. I couldn't pass it up. This was an opportunity for me to rub shoulders with Lisa Nichols and learn how to create a speaking business that could potentially make millions. So, I jumped on a plane and went to California. While I was gone the agent called and said the title work was ready and the owner's daughter was ready to close the deal. Well I couldn't possibly close the deal while I was in California, so I called one of my investor friends and gave him the opportunity to get a good deal for $195,000. He looked at the property, reviewed the comparable sales for the area and quickly determined this was a deal. So, we agreed on an assignment fee of $10,000. So, while I was in California attending a conference, I was negotiating a wholesale deal with another investor. We agreed on the terms, executed an assignment of contract with a fee of $10,000. We closed the deal as soon as I got back, and I collected a check for $10,000 wholesaling a property to another investor.

What is Wholesaling?

To decide whether flipping properties or holding them long-term is the more appropriate strategy, you will need to answer a few critical questions.

First, decide whether the funds will be used to build a residential portfolio that creates residual income or allocated to fund a larger investment such as an apartment complex or commercial building.

I personally believe buying and holding real estate for the long term is one of the most effective wealth building strategies available to the general population. Here are my top 10 reasons why I like this model:

1.) Appreciation

Despite the recent real estate crash, when you look at real estate over the long haul, it's accurate to assume some level of appreciation in your real estate holdings. Yes, there are market cycles where values rise quickly or fall quickly, but by and large, real estate is an asset class that appreciates. In addition to this, investors can research market dynamics and make knowledgeable decisions based on anticipated appreciation for a market.

2.) Passive Income

Once you have made the decision to buy and hold or fix and flip you are ready to get started investing.

Holding real estate can be a very passive investment that provides returns much higher than could be obtained through other passive investments (ie. stock, bonds, etc.). With the ability to outsource property management, accounting, etc., investors can still make good returns while playing a very hands-off roll in the investment.

3.) High Leverage

Real estate investing is one of the few investment vehicles with the availability of high leverage (i.e. financing). Try walking into your local bank and asking for a line of credit for $800,000 secured against only $200,000 of your cash for investing in gold, stocks, mutual funds, commodities, etc. They would probably laugh at you. But, if you walked into that same bank and told them you wanted to buy 10 houses at $100,000 a piece .... they would usher you over into their mortgage division to begin working on your 10 loans.

4.) High ROI

With the ability to acquire high leverage comes the ability to obtain a very high return on investment. Not only does your monthly cash on cash return go way up when you use leverage, any appreciation on the property amplifies your ROI as well. This is because the entire asset appreciates rather than just the amount of money you invested as a down payment.

5.) Principle Pay Down

A commonly overlooked benefit of investing in real estate is the fact that while your tenant may provide you with positive cash flow above and beyond your mortgage payment, they are also helping to pay down the mortgage as well. While the principle portion of the mortgage payment is minimal at first, every year that you own the property the amortization of the principle amount of your loan speeds up. Before long, you are shaving thousands of dollars from your loan amount every year until ultimately you own the property outright.

6.) Tax Benefits

As taxpayers in a tightening tax system, any kind of deduction can be helpful. Owning real estate allows for the deduction of mortgage insurance as well as the depreciation of the property itself. In addition to this, real estate can also afford you the opportunity to defer tax liability by using 1031 exchanges to continue investing funds in new properties while deferring tax liability indefinitely.

7.) Hedge Against Inflation

Many analysts believe inflation is coming (if not already here). Owning real estate and using leverage (especially at these low interest rates) is a great way to hedge against coming inflation. If prices rise, so will the cost of housing ... owning an asset that rises with the tied is a great way to protect your wealth.

8.) Increasing Rents

Very few would speculate that housing rents will decrease over time. Most analysts have already stated that rents are expected to increase over the coming years. Owning real estate not only allows you to lock in housing prices and interest rates that are at all-time lows, it also provides you with an opportunity to increase future cash flows by increasing rents ... thus increasing your ROI in future years.

9.) Retirement Income

For those investors that look at real estate investing as a very long-term proposition, the potential to retire on rental income is very real. I know many investors that have owned real estate for multiple decades as a retirement strategy and ended up very wealthy as a result. Over a 20-30-year period, investors can own numerous properties outright and create a net worth well into the millions. Additionally, the cash-flow that can be generated from properties that no longer have mortgages can be very nice supplements to pensions, 401Ks, social security, etc.

10.) Creative Exits

One of the best characteristics of real estate investing is the plethora of strategies that can be employed when selling a property. Real estate is nice because it doesn't have to be a permanent proposition. You can own a property for 1 month or 50 years ... it's completely up to you. When it comes time to sell a property, investors can use any number of different strategies to maximize profits.

Let's begin by explaining each method:

Buy & Hold

It is a well-known fact that buying and holding real estate is a recipe for amassing great wealth. Most "old money" in the U.S. and abroad was accumulated through land ownership. Even after periods of decreasing land prices, land values have almost always rebounded in the long run because there is a limited supply of land. Therefore, people investing in land as a general rule is always a good idea.

A buy & hold real estate investor must have property and people management skills to be successful holding real estate. Many investors, especially first-time rental property owners, are ill-prepared or ill-equipped to deal with the responsibilities that come with managing rental property. The process of finding quality tenants and servicing their needs, along with ensuring the maintenance and upkeep of the property, can be a stressful and time-intensive undertaking. Therefore, successful property and people management is necessary for ensuring ongoing cash flows from real estate investments. Take note that property management services charge fees to use their services, but they are worth the investment to manage your investments and properties, so you do not have to take the added time and effort to do that. Additionally, they have an expertise that many first-time property owners do not have when it comes to rentals and servicing rental properties.

Fix & Flip Properties

Investors that focus on fix and flip properties usually look for distressed properties by identifying homeowners who can no longer manage or sustain their properties. These can also be identified through foreclosure properties as well. Investors looking to Fix & Flip will remodel or enhance a property so that it works better for homeowners or is more efficient for apartment tenants. Using this tactic, the buyer of a fixer is relying on investing capital to increase values as opposed to just buying property for a low basis to create high investment returns.

The most apparent advantage to flipping property investments is the ability to immediately realize gains and to have capital tied up for the least amount of time possible.

Flipping properties should be considered more of a tactical strategy rather than a long-term investment strategy. Because transaction costs are very high on both the buy and sell side, they can significantly affect profits.

Also, it is important to assess the possible income gain from the Fix & Flip strategy on each purchase. Some homes will have a greater margin for profit than others. There are many factors that will contribute to this such as the desirability of the neighborhood, the amount of work needed to be done, and the approximate resale value. With this it is important to evaluate in advance the construction or contractor costs which would also be added to the cost of the single home purchase. Then the sell value would subtract these costs to determine the approximate profit.

Conclusion

Although the choice between the Buy & Hold or Fix and Flip strategies depends on your financial situation and investment goals, the Buy & Hold strategy is generally more appropriate for those using real estate as a core portion of their overall investment portfolios.

Fix & Flipping properties is more appropriate when real estate is used as a method to acquire large amounts of cash. Investors wishing to amass wealth and to derive income from their real estate investments should consider holding real estate for the long term, using the equity built into the portfolio to finance other investment opportunities, with the potential of eventually selling the properties in an up market.

Flipping properties is a tactic that is best suited for periods when prospects in the stock and bond markets are low, or for investors wishing to realize short-term capital gains for as long as the present market will allow.

It would also be important for flippers to have a good relationship with a contractor or construction firm that they trust to handle the upgrades, remodel or enhancements unless the investor plans to do the work him/herself.

CHAPTER 8 ACTION STEPS

Reposition Yourself

To reposition yourself I am recommending the following action steps:

1. Assess your current financial picture. Determine where you stand and determine where you want to be by the end of year. Make decisions, make a vision board and begin taking massive actions.

2. Determine which strategy will be best for your financial situation. Wholesaling, Fixing and Flipping or Buy and Holds.

3. Hire a mentor and coach to help you with the accountability of your decisions.

CHAPTER 9
ROAD TO RICHES INVESTING IN COMMERCIAL REAL ESTATE

Many people start out investing in residential real estate simply because they're more accustomed to buying homes, but commercial real estate can be a great way to balance your portfolio. You just need to sharpen your saw on the different rules and terms in the commercial market.

First let's look at the differences in residential vs commercial.

Residential Vs. Commercial

Commercial real estate is valued differently. The income that a piece of commercial real estate produces is directly related to its usable square footage. This isn't always the case with residential. Residential real estate can be valued by the school zones, the desirability of the district or neighborhood.

Commercial property helps diversify risk. For example, if you own an apartment building and you lose one of your 10 tenants, you only lose one-tenth of the income for that property, instead of the entire rent as you would if you lost a tenant in a single-family house. Therefore, you have more leverage with a commercial property.

Cash flow is often greater with commercial real estate. The yield is often higher per square foot and on an initial investment basis than it is in residential. If you lease or rent a multi-unit commercial property, you have more tenants to generate income than you do with a single-family dwelling. This multiplies your income which you can then use to pay the mortgage or invest in other properties to increase your portfolio.

Commercial real estate leases are generally much longer. This helps with the stability of your cash flow. Also, as stated earlier, commercial real estate tenants are more likely than residential tenants to pay regularly and on time.

Commercial property is valued by the bank differently. You'll need to find a bank that works with commercial real estate (most major lenders do), and it'll want a higher down payment than for residential property--usually 30 percent or more.

What are Commercial Properties?

Commercial properties may refer to:

> - retail buildings
> - office buildings
> - warehouses
> - industrial buildings
> - apartment buildings
> - "mixed use" buildings, where the property may have a mix, such as retail, office and apartments

Some of the largest real estate fortunes are earned in commercial real estate.

That is, buildings and other facilities in which your tenants are there to earn money in the space they rent from you.

Commercial real estate is ALL business. That is why it is much easier to run than residential real estate where people live in your building. Your tenants treat you as a fellow business person. So, they pay their rent on time, allow you time to make any needed repairs, do not bug you on weekends, etc.

Let's explore options for investing in commercial real estate:

The common key metrics to use for when assessing real estate include:

Net Operating Income (NOI)

The NOI or Net Operating Income of a commercial real estate property is calculated by evaluating the property's first year gross operating income and then subtracting the operating expenses for the first year. You want to have a positive NOI. It is also important to establish (if you are purchasing commercial properties) whether this includes parking and services fees (such as laundry or vending for example). Also, it is important to note that the NOI is a before tax calculation and does not include depreciation, amortization, capital expenditures, or interest and principal payments on loans.

Cap Rate

A real estate property's "cap" – or capitalization – rate, is used to calculate the value of income producing properties. For example, an apartment complex of five units or more, commercial office buildings, and smaller strip malls are all good candidates for a cap rate determination. Cap rates are used to estimate the net present value of future profits or cash flow; the process is also called capitalization of earnings. More specifically, the cash flow is determined by net operating income (after expenses) or the income generated by rentals for example. Then this number is divided by the purchase amount to determine the capitalization rate.

Cash on Cash

Commercial real estate investors who rely on financing to purchase their properties often adhere to the cash-on-cash formula to compare first-year performance of competing properties. Cash-on-cash takes the fact that the investor in question doesn't require 100% cash to buy the property into account, but also accounts for the fact that the investor will not keep all the NOI (Net Operating Income) because he or she must use some of it to make mortgage payments. To uncover cash on cash, real estate investors must determine the amount required to invest to purchase the property, or their initial investment.

Advantages of Investing in Small Multi Family Apartments

Smaller multifamily properties can provide an investor some of the strongest investment opportunities if you know what you are looking for. You can find them everywhere, and often can buy them for much higher immediate returns and at better purchase terms than larger properties.

We define smaller multifamily properties as those having four to 100 apartments or units. This size of property can be a great fit for individual or a small group of investors. At this size, the income can adequately cover the expenses of the property and factor in management, debt service, and vacancy expenses.

Some of the advantages of investing in smaller multifamily properties are:

> Smaller properties usually have less competition than larger properties. When acquiring smaller properties, you are usually competing against individual investors instead of large companies, institutional investors, or investment groups.

> You can find properties with higher cash on cash returns. Often you can buy smaller properties that provide higher cash on cash and internal rates of return on your investment dollars.

> They take less equity to purchase. Because they are smaller, they don't require millions of dollars in equity to purchase, allowing you to purchase them individually or with a small group of investors, and own a higher percentage of the property.

> With smaller properties, you can often make more money per unit each month than with bigger properties.

> There are more of them in your backyard. There is a larger number of smaller properties than large apartment complexes which makes them easier to find.

➢ Many have more flexible sellers. These properties are normally owned by private individuals who can get creative if they want to and don't have to go to a large ownership group for approval.

➢ They are often managed by less sophisticated investors who are scared to raise rents, fearing that their tenants will move out. This provides more opportunities for hands-on owners to achieve management improvements and value creation.

➢ They can be closed on quicker than larger properties.

Top 10 Reasons to Buy Multifamily

When you sit down and examine the advantage of owning multifamily properties, you will be amazed at the multitude of benefits. While other avenues of income generation offer some attractive incentives, owning multifamily properties brings many great things to the table. Let us explore these advantages:

1. You can outsource your property management to professionals. You don't have to be bothered by tenants and toilets. Even if you have smaller properties, you can hire property managers. Leave the headaches to them and go on vacation! The property doesn't own you; you own the property.

2. You can buy with NONE of your own cash. You can raise private money to cover any cash requirements. You will find that it's easier to get financing on apartments and that the MORE you borrow the LESS they look at the borrower's credit. In some instances, they don't even look at the borrower's credit but at the borrower's assets instead.

3. Apartments are made to cash flow even with nothing down. This means that instead of there being one house with one roof generating only one source of income, you have one roof with possibly multiple apartments under it creating multiple income streams. You have economy to scale. Apartments are designed to be income-producing properties.

4. Better leverage of your time and effort. Think about it. What would you rather do? Look for ten houses or a ten-unit apartment building? On the flip side, wouldn't you rather sell a ten-unit apartment than sell ten houses? Of course! You have more leverage of your time.

5. The value of income properties is based on income. This is a function of Net Operating Income (NOI) and you can create value by raising the rents and cutting the expenses. This is a very predictable process. You can determine how much the property is worth based on how much you raise the rents.

6. Less competition. There are less people out doing multifamily deals than single family deals because they lack mindset and they lack specialized knowledge. They have limited themselves by the mindset that says they must graduate from single-family homes to multifamily properties.

7. There is less risk. With multiple tenants you have multiple revenue streams. If you lose one client, it's not the end of your business. On the other hand, if you are relying on a house as your sole source of income and you lose that tenant, you are still pouring money into that house. There is mitigated risk through apartments.

8. Non-recourse financing. The more money you borrow, the easier it is to borrow. When you get to loans of two million dollars and above, it becomes non-recourse financing which means the asset is the sole security for the loan. No one is personally guaranteeing the loan.

9. Condo conversion. This has been very big in some parts of the country such as Denver and Tampa. As an example, you would take a five plex, convert it into condos, and then sell the individual units. It is a different strategy because you're putting all your cash forward and then pulling out. It's not a long-term hold strategy.

10. The subprime lender bust. With subprime mortgage lenders falling out of the market, there are people cannot qualify for home loans. These people must live somewhere so the demand for rentals is skyrocketing.

As you can see, the advantages to owning multifamily properties are solid and sound. With so many venues to consider when trying to find something to generate passive income for yourself, you just can't overlook the tremendous value created by multifamily properties.

Qualifying & Analyzing Apartment Deals

Determining the value of an apartment building investment is one of the greatest difficulties that many new commercial real estate investors face.

Most people who invest in apartments have some experience investing in other types of real estate, typically residential homes or duplexes and triplexes. The issue that new investors face is the fact that apartment buildings are valued by different methods than residential real estate. In fact, it is usually quite easy to find the fair value of residential estate using a comparative sales approach. The comparative sales approach simply uses the existing sales prices of similar residential properties in that area and determines value based on an average sales price of comparable properties. This should be very straight forward.

However, commercial real estate investors and appraisers use a variety of appraisal methods to determine the fair market value of an apartment building. These new methods should not deter the new investor because once they are understood they will help tremendously to locate the best apartment building for acquisition.

The first unfamiliar term that a new apartment building buyer will encounter is the capitalization rate or CAP rate for short.

As the new investor is searching for an apartment building the Realtor will supply the CAP rate of the property. The CAP rate is a measure of the income produced by an apartment building divided by the cost of the building.

For example: if an apartment building is purchased for the price of $1,000,000.00 and the property produced an annual net operating income of $100,000.00 the CAP rate of the property is 10%. (Net operating income is gross rents minus expenses.)

Net Operating Income: $100,000.00
Purchase Price: $1,000,000.00
CAP rate =   10%

An investor can also use the CAP rate to determine the maximum price he can pay for a property when he knows what the net operating income is.

For example, if the investor is looking at an apartment building that is seeing a net operating income of $150,000.00 and he wants to see a CAP rate of 11% he can determine the maximum purchase price as follows:

Net Operating Income: $150,000.00
CAP Rate: 11%
Maximum purchase price: $1,363.636.00

This simple formula to devise the capitalization rate (CAP rate) of an apartment building is limited. The simple CAP rate assumes that the investor will be purchasing the property for cash and does not consider the financing terms that will affect the investor's rate of return on the building.

In other words, the simple CAP rate is good number to use when comparing apartment buildings as potential investments but a little bit more analysis is necessary to determine exactly what the true rate of return will be on a building when using financing to purchase the property.

The goal for the individual investor is to determine what the property is worth to him or her. In other words, the investor should only be concerned with paying a price for the property that allows him to realize his sought-after rate of return.

The best way that I have found to determine the investment value of an apartment building is to use the "Band of Equity Investment Method".

The "Band of Equity Investment Method" of determining value will tell you the maximum price that you can pay for your apartment building and still realize the rate of return that you are looking for.

The greatest advantage of this valuation formula is that it takes into consideration the terms of financing that the investor is using to purchase the property.

Thankfully, this method is not that complicated, and it merely requires that you know some financial information about the property and the terms of the financing that you will using.

Here is how the "Band of Equity Investment Method" is figured:

Mortgage:

Loan to Value of Mortgage x Mortgage Constant = ____

Property:

Down Payment on Property (as a percentage) x Desired Rate of Return = ____

Mortgage :	80% (.80) X 7.99% (.0799) = 0.06 +
Equity :	20% (.20) X 11% (.11) = 0.02
Cap Rate:	.06+.02= 0.08 = 8.0%

With this new "derived" CAP rate you can now determine your maximum purchase price for any apartment building and ensure that you will be realizing at least an 11% rate of return on your investment.

For example, you are out looking at 14-unit apartment building with your realtor and he tells you that the net operating is $150,000.00. You know that your bank will give you a 30-year loan at an interest rate of 7.99%. You know that you need to see at least an 11% return on your investment.

You simply divide $150,000.00 by your derived CAP rate of 8% and you get the price of $1,875,000.00. You know that you can purchase the building with a 20% down payment and a 30-year loan at 7.99% and still realize a net return of 11% on your investment.

How to Find Apartment Deals

If you're wholesaling apartment buildings, your job is finding deals. Not just good deals, great deals. This is what makes wholesaling work–deals so good that investors act fast to take them off the market, before other investors snatch them up.

The ideal market for this is one where there are plenty of properties available to buy and growing investor demand. This situation is most commonly found in markets that are transitioning from a downturn or depressed economic state to an expansion.

There are a quite a few ways to source multi-family deals, but these two approaches will provide you a steady flow of great deals that you can either flip for cash or buy and hold for cash flow.

Commercial Brokers

Brokers are a good source of deals, though mainly in down markets. In hot markets, the money is flowing, and brokers take on a Master of The Universe attitude, making them difficult to deal with. Properties are selling at list–or being bid up. They don't need you.

When a market correction comes though, the situation reverses. Banks outsource the liquidation of their REOs (Real Estate Owned) to asset managers, who in turn engage brokers, and there are waves of multi-family REO listings. Supply exceeds demand, and they need your help to turn the properties back into cash.

Most brokers have made unrealistic promises to an asset manager as to what price they can bring in, so they are going to carry on with hardball inflexibility on price the first time you contact them.

What puts the negotiation in your favor is... the numbers. There are so many other properties on the market ready to be liquidated that the market just won't support the price the broker wants you to pay. Eventually (if they want to sell) the price must come down.

Here's how this plays out in reality...

Buyer #1 offers list price, but after two months he finds he can't raise the money, and the deal falls out of escrow. The broker is unhappy, but believes it was a flaky buyer at fault, not too high a price.

Three weeks later, Buyer #2 offers 95% of list price. But again, seven weeks into the contract the buyer backs out, unable to raise financing. The broker is disappointed and starting to lose some face, but he still blames "buyers." He talks with the asset manager and lowers the list price by 10%.

This scenario plays itself out two more times, and the listing is about to expire a second time. The broker now feels there's nothing to lose and advises the asset manager that: Due to market conditions, only a large price reduction will sell the property. He gets the OK.

Throughout this whole period, you have stayed in touch with the broker, knowing what you can pay and calling every two weeks to see if the property is available at that price. You may have made first contact during Buyer #1 or during Buyer #4.

Regardless, your professionalism, and relentless bi-weekly follow up contact puts you on the broker's radar and ever closer to be the "go to" investor when price finally comes down.

Finally, the day arrives when the broker learns that Buyer #4 is not going to close. The broker may reach out and call you. If not, you catch the fact in your regular follow up. Now, with the seller and broker sufficiently smacked around by the market, both are motivated and open to an offer at your price.

You make the offer; it's accepted. You easily find a buyer who pays you a six-figure assignment fee for the opportunity to take over the property, stabilize it, and lock in seven figures in equity and a five-figure net monthly positive cash flow.

Play this contact and follow up activity out over five to ten brokers, and you have a steady flow of deals in development and coming to fruition. Over time, your reputation with brokers becomes gold plated, and deals start finding their way to you.

Brokers offer high leverage and working them as above puts you in the path of great deals, one after the other. When the market heats up and the expansion phase gathers momentum, broker-sourced deals start to dry up. To tap into the broader pool of sellers (not serviced by brokers), you need other tools.

One of the most effective is direct mail.

You can get a list of all the apartment buildings in your county from the County Assessor. You can segment that list in several ways to uncover motivated apartment property owners needing a buyer to take their problem of their hands.

1. Out-of-Town Owners. One way to segment the list is to sort it for out-of-town owners. They're inherently motivated sellers due to their distance from the property, lack of control, and high cost of doing anything about it.

Now you may think that this is obvious, but the truth is most people don't like to spend the money it takes to put a mailing together and get it out. The funny thing is, most of us don't blink at the $100 it costs for dinner and a movie, yet when it comes to investing $50-100 in a mailing campaign to get motivated sellers calling with deals that will yield five or six figures in profit, we balk.

As a result, these owners remain under-serviced, and the demand for buyers who can help them remains high. This will remain a great place for you to start looking for deals if people balk at the $50-100 required to put out a postcard campaign—i.e. forever.

2. Segment by size. Another way to segment the list is by apartment size. Most assessors have size range designations they put each property in. For example: 5-19 units, 20-40 units, and 40+ units in the case of my local county.

Once you have the list segmented into your desired target markets, mail them a postcard or letter quarterly. To stay busy, rotate through your different segments, one per month.

The result is a steady flow of apartment owners (at various stages of motivation) calling you to find out if you can help them out of their situation.

For each call you get, take the seller through a Lead Conversion Process that screens for motivation, the deal criteria you're looking for, and floats an offer to the seller that provides a solution to the problem that's driving them to call you.

If there's firm interest, you proceed with closing. If the seller is interested, but not yet ready to go forward, put them on your follow-up list and stay in touch until they ready to sell on your terms or sell to someone else.

The qualifier for your following up with a seller is motivation—a factor in their situation that requires they sell. By following up with sellers who have genuine motivation driving them (partner dispute, inherited property, out-of-control management), you develop a pipeline of deals.

While there are other effective ways to source great multi-family deals, commercial brokers and direct mail are the two approaches you can count on to produce reliable results.

#1 Secret to Raising Private Money for Apartments

The secret to getting financial commitments from investors long before you have your first deal under contract is to … make up a deal.

You "make up a deal" by creating a "Sample Deal Package". This document contains everything about your fictitious deal including photos, information about the building and area, actual financials, your business plan, projected financials and returns. You will use this Sample Deal Package to speak with potential investors. You will even use it to build credibility with other professionals you're trying to recruit to your team (like commercial real estate brokers, lenders, insurance agents, attorneys etc.).

The difference between a Sample Deal Package and a real one is that all the information about the deal is accurate (photos, location, financials, etc.), except that you don't have it under contract. The other difference is that your fictitious purchase price may be lower than the asking price so that you achieve the desired returns for the investors. In other words, you approach your potential investors with a deal package that looks like the real thing.

How to create a Sample Deal Package?

Find and re-purpose the marketing package for a listed property and turn that into your Sample Deal Package. It will contain an executive summary about the building, investment terms and potential returns; information about the building and area; photos; actual financials; projected financials; potential estimated returns for the investors; and information about yourself and your team.

Where do you get all this information?

One good (free) source is www.loopnet.com, which lets you search for the kind of deals you want to do. Download a good marketing package and get to work.

Having this Sample Deal Package does several things for you:

1. It allows you to better visualize your deal.

This is critical as you expand your own comfort zone with doing your first commercial real estate deal or doing bigger ones than before. Seeing the photos, visiting the property, writing and talking about it make this deal real for you. The more real it seems to you, the more comfortable you become and the more confidently you can talk about it.

2. It empowers you to get started now.

You can now schedule meetings with potential investors and say, "I don't have a deal right now, but when I do, it'll look substantially like this" and then you show them the Sample Deal Package. It gives you something to talk about today.

3. It will allow you to get financial commitments from your investors long before you have a deal under contract.

By the time you get a building under contract, you've already primed your investors and received financial commitments based on a deal substantially like that in the Sample Deal Package. When you have a property under contract, you will send your investors the real Deal Package, re-confirm their commitment and close on time.

Creating a Sample Deal Package allows you to get started NOW with apartment building investing. It allows you to better visualize your deal, gives you the confidence to make offers, and secures commitments from your investors long before you put your first property under contract, so you can close on time.

How to Make Quick Cash Wholesaling Apartments

If you are looking to make some quick cash to build up your cash account, wholesaling apartments can be a great way to start the process.

Wholesaling Multifamily Properties

The real estate market is roaring back! And today's market can be good news for wholesalers who learn to capitalize on these opportunities.

One of the primary reason's prices are escalating fast is because of the reduced bottom-feeder inventory of cheap houses, because of the drastically declining inventory of foreclosures. The very best foreclosure deals are routinely receiving a bidding war and only the highest bidder gets to buy the house.

A myth about wholesaling real estate is that it only works on single-family "junker" houses. Wholesaling works with all asset classes of real estate including single family, duplex, multi-family, mobile homes, commercial, land, etc.

The Wholesaling Process

Wholesaling is the process of finding great real estate deals, writing a contract to acquire the deal, and then selling the contract to another buyer. Generally, a wholesaler never actually owns the piece of property they are selling; instead, a wholesaler simply finds great deals using a variety of marketing strategies, puts them under contract, and sells that contract to another for an "assignment fee."

This fee is typically between $500 and $5,000 on average or more depending on the size of the deal. Essentially, the wholesaler is a middleman who is paid for finding deals.

Some wholesalers sell their contracts to retail buyers, but most sell their contracts to other investors (often house flippers) who are typically "cash buyers." When dealing with these cash buyers, a wholesaler can often get paid within days or weeks and can build solid connections in the real estate community.

Many investors choose to begin with wholesaling due to its reputation of being an easy strategy and one with low startup costs when first beginning. Because the property is never actually owned by the wholesaler, there are no rehab costs, loan fees, contractors, tenants, banks, or other complications. Wholesaling is the most popular strategy taught by real estate gurus and often receives the most attention as a result, though it is not as easy to become a successful wholesaler as they make it sound.

Wholesalers must continually seek out the best deals to have inventory to sell to others and must have a well-designed marketing funnel to continually attract these leads.

Wholesalers also must continually seek out buyers for the deals they acquire. While promoted as a strategy that anyone can do -- even someone with ZERO money -- you ultimately do need to have financial resources to build your marketing funnel. That said, those who persist in growing their wholesaling skills often find great success and a good source of income while they grow their knowledge of other, more profitable strategies.

CHAPTER 9 ACTION STEPS

Reposition Yourself

Locating Multi Family Apartments to Invest or Wholesale

1. Visit Loopnet.com and search for apartments for sale. Make contact with the listing broker and request all information

2. Build a sample deal package and begin to talk to financial advisers, tax preparers and mortgage bankers to request funding for your deal.

3. Wholesaling Apartments- If you decide to wholesale the units instead of investing yourself, build a buyers list by advertising for cash buyers

CHAPTER 10
UNLIMITED RESIDUAL INCOME IN
NEW CONSTRUCTION INVESTING

Clients often ask me what my thoughts are about investing in new construction homes purchased from the builder or developer. As with most other nuances of real estate investing, this strategy has its pros and cons. A prudent real estate investor needs to clearly understand what they are and how they can potentially impact their success. Then and only then, that investor can determine if this strategy is a good fit with their long-term goals.

Let's talk about the pros and cons of investing in new construction.

Pros of investing in new construction homes

Investing in new homes reduces maintenance over time

Inexperienced investors without proper guidance often disregard this principle at their own peril. If you think that the built-in equity more than makes up for the fact that the home was built when Mick Jagger was a chap, I have a bridge to sell you in Alaska. The fact is, if you invest in a new home today, ten years later, that home is just ten years old.

Obvious, I know. But it's critical in the context of long-term investing. As you are executing your long-term

Blueprint, it is important that maintenance issues don't undo the good progress you make increasing your capital base.

Builders incentives can be used to lower the capital invested

To drive sales, Builders sometimes offer flexible incentives that can allow a real estate investor to limit his cash out of pocket investment to just the down payment. For instance, the asking price on a new construction property I showed last week was $133k but the Builder was offering $16k in incentives to be used however the investor sees fit.

My advice to the client was to use about a fourth of that amount to cover closing costs and apply the rest toward the purchase price. That way he cuts his out of pocket investment by 30%. That doesn't sound like much, but it would allow the investor to purchase an additional home for every four homes acquired and that's worth hundreds of thousands in the long run.

Ample supply avoids bidding wars and frustration

Unlike foreclosures or short sale listings, well priced inventory homes are plentiful, so the investor can focus on which asset offers the best package of location, price, amenities and incentives, instead of getting into an ego war with twelve other bidders. The ability to acquire assets on demand can make a world of difference if say, you miss buying that house because you were chasing that great foreclosure deal that never materialized. Or if you missed out on that low interest rate for the same reason.

Buying new offers convenience and faster turnaround

When you close on a new home, you can swap the builders sign for a "For Lease" sign that same day. If instead you opt for a distressed type asset, chances are some repairs will need to be completed prior to the home being rent ready. No matter how cosmetic they might be, they do take time and they take time away from the property being available for showing to tenants. The overall process is more seamless, and the experience is drastically better especially for a first-time real estate investor.

Higher quality new construction attracts higher quality tenants

In my experience, high quality new construction homes with upgrades such as granite, stainless appliances and energy star ratings tend to attract higher quality tenants that won't mind paying premium rent. So instead of renting an average property for average rent you offer a premium property for premium rent. Plus, this type of tenant tends to have higher credit scores, stable employments and won't mind signing longer term leases. Plus, offering a property that is under builder warranty on most items for 1-2 years is a big plus to them as well. And finally, 10 years from now, that higher quality will translate to higher appreciation and ultimately higher returns.

Cons of investing in new construction homes

Paying retail prices

Even after taking into consideration the "rich" incentives builders offer, the price you ultimately pay for the property is the retail market value of the home or close to it. Some investors are bothered by that fact even though to a long-term real estate investor equity doesn't matter because it's just an indication of what would happen if you sold the property right now. Essentially you are trading off money for time: you are paying a little more for the home, but you are gaining a seamless, hassle free process. Also, paying retail prices makes the investor more susceptible to strong emotions during market cycles.

Here's what I mean: Many out of state investors (primarily from California) purchased new homes from builders at the top of the market in 2003-2005 for $120-$130k. Five years later, bank owned properties next to them were selling for 20-30k less. Things have stabilized in those neighborhoods now, but it was hard to see that coming in 08 when it was all doom and gloom. So, the investor must truly be committed to the investment long term to ride out market value swings. Remember, the only market value that matters, is the one when you sell. The rest is just fiction.

The Unknowns

When you purchase a home that was built 4-5 years ago, you know exactly what the property taxes will be in the coming year and you can run your cash flow analysis with certainty. In new construction homes, the first year you own the property taxes are very low since the property is being taxes just on the land. The following year you don't know for certain what the county will appraise the property for tax purposes, so you must estimate it. However, there are certain steps we can take to limit this uncertainty. Worst case scenario, the taxes will be the price paid for the property times the tax rate which is known at the time of purchase. Typically, though, the country appraisal for tax purposes is lower than the price paid for the property. So, we can run several scenarios and see if the deal makes sense. Lastly, we can see examples of properties sold by the Builder in the past couple of years and check the tax valuations of those homes for a clearer idea.

Investing in new construction homes certainly has its positives and negatives. But for the real estate investor that understands them, that has a well laid out long term Blueprint and has the discipline to execute the plan it can be a very successful strategy.

How to Create Unlimited Income Investing in New Construction

Creating unlimited income investing in new construction or any real property is one of the fastest ways to consistent and reliable income. The first questions you should ask yourself is what you want to achieve and why. After you do that, you need to figure out HOW to do it.

Let's say your goal is to generate $5,000 per month in passive income from your real estate investments. How will you get there? How many rental houses or apartment building units will you need?

Here's a step-by-step methodology to answer this, followed by a more detailed case study to illustrate the concept.

How to Create $5,000/Month in Passive Income

Step #1: Create a Realistic Financial Model

The first thing you need is a financial model you can use to forecast the projected cash flow for a property over the life of the project. For income, you should have line items for rental income, but also account for concessions, vacancies and delinquencies. For expenses, include property management expenses (if applicable), real estate taxes, insurance, repairs and maintenance, utilities, trash and snow removal, landscaping, and legal expenses.

Step #2: Determine the Projected Cash Flow Per Unit

Once you have a financial model, then it's time to populate it with data. To get the data, you will need to do some research and use some assumptions. The more data and research you do, the more accurate your projections will be. As sources for your data, talk to other landlords and brokers about their rents and expenses. If you're looking at apartment buildings, review lots of marketing packages to get a sense for the potential cash flow of a property.

Create a financial model for as many houses or apartment buildings you can find. Then create ONE financial model with an average of all of these.

This one financial model will tell you how much cash flow to expect from a single rental property or a single unit in an apartment building.

What you're looking for is the Expected Cash Flow of One Unit.

Step #3: Calculate the Number of Units You Need to Achieve Your Goal

The last step is easy. To answer the question "how many units do I need to generate $5,000 of income per month," use this formula:

\# Units Needed = $5,000 / Expected Cash Flow of One Unit

Let's look at a sample real estate investment:

This example will be based on a 21-unit newly constructed condominium building.

If I examine the 5-year Profit and Loss statement of my deal analyzer model and divide the total cash flow per month by the number of units, I get the following cash flow per unit per month:

Cash Flow Per Unit Per Month

Year 1	Year 2	Year 3	Year 4	Year 5	Average
$124	$224	$297	$316	$335	$259

As we increase the rents, the cash flow per unit also increases.

Let's see how many units we need to purchase to generate $5,000 per month:

# of Units to Achieve $5000 Per Month

Year 1	Year 2	Year 3	Year 4	Year 5	Average
$124	$224	$297	$316	$335	$259
40	22	17	16	15	19

In Year 1, when cash flow per unit per month is $124, we would need 40 units like that to generate $5,000. This building is only 21-units, so to achieve our goal of $5,000, we would need to purchase two of these buildings.

However, look at Year 2. In Year 2 the cash flow is now $224 per month per unit because we have been able to raise the rents a bit. Based on that cash flow, we would need 22 units like that to achieve our goal of $5,000.

This happens to be a 21-unit so we're already there! Our income is $5,000 per month!

As we reach our goal of raising the rents of ALL the units by $100 after Year 3, our cash flow continues to increase.

CHAPTER 10 ACTION STEPS

Reposition Yourself

You can invest in new construction projects that will generate residual income by first determining the amount of income you want to generate each month. Once you have determined the income complete the following activity to reposition yourself.

1. Research and locate builders in the area you want to invest in. Take the time to visit the communities.

2. Get a list of their inventory and ask about any pricing incentives.

3. Research and review the rental comps for the area to determine if you will be able to lease the properties and at what rental rates.

4. If you are going to finance the properties, consult a mortgage banker or private lender to secure the financing and terms.

5. Review the numbers and analyze if you should invest in the properties based on the monthly payment and the potential rental income

6. Execute the contract to purchase

7. Pre-lease by hiring a property manager to market for new tenants or begin to advertise in the local newspaper or on social media.

8. Select and prescreen the tenants, obtain applications and initial deposits

9. Close on the loan with the lender and allow the tenants to move in

10. Collect your residual income monthly

CASH FLOW FOR BUSINESS OWNERS

FAST EASY AND RELIABLE STEPS FOR SMALL BUSINESS OWNERS TO CREATE RESIDUAL INCOME INVESTING

7 FAST EASY AND RELIABLE STEPS FOR SMALL BUSINESS OWNERS TO CREATE RESIDUAL INCOME INVESTING

Step 1: Mastermind Group for Next Level Thinking

There is an adage "You are who you hang around". The people who you spend most of your time with become your circle of influence. They will rub off on you and you will rub off on them. If you were to take the average income of the 5 people that influence you most, that's your income as well. If they are broke, then so are you. If they are rich, you will be too. Are you associated with a mastermind group that offers next level thinking or a group that undermines your every move to keep you grounded? It is important that you assess who you spend your time with and then evaluate who you want to spend your time with. Spend more time with individuals that will challenge your thinking and assist with getting you to the next level. If your mastermind group does not offer you the level of Think and Grow Rich thinking that you need, find another group. Make new friends. Find a new circle of influence. This is how you will grow beyond your wildest dreams.

Also, maybe you are not ready to distance yourself from friends and family who are not in the right mindset. Instead add people to your circle who are success minded and hang out with them more. Encourage your old friends or family to do the same. Just like Ghandi said, "Be the change you want to see in the world." So, in this way add more successful people to your circle and help those who need to be success minded getting there. My mission has been to pass it on and pay it forward, so instead of letting others bring me down, I am doing my best to lift others up.

Step 2 Systemize Your Why

A key component to reaching your definite major purpose is to define your why. Your why is the reason you are doing the job or providing the service or products. It is the reason you get up and continuously go to work every day. Once you identify your why you should write it down and review it daily. My strategy is to keep a notebook of my why. I use this notebook daily for journaling and keeping track of my goals and my purpose. Using the same notebook can help you for staying organized and assists in keeping your systems in place.

Recently, I attended The Small Business Expo in Dallas, Texas and was privileged to attend one of the workshops that ask the infamous question. Why are you doing what you are doing? What you are doing? I thought about it and said to myself because this is all I know how to do. If this is all I know how to do, and I am an expert in my industry, what is the reason I am not seeing the results? Why I am not living out my dreams. Why am I not financially free?

So, ask yourself this question – Why are you doing what you are doing? Why did you decide to pick up this book? Clearly you want a greater Cash Flow. But what is your why? Expand on this.

Your why is one of the most important aspects of your decision to operate a successful business long term. You must create systems for your business that will automate the work processes and allow you the time to analyze new ways to create Cash Flow that can be used to invest in other opportunities such as real estate. In Robert Kyosaki's Cash Flow Quadrant he talks about the roles of an employee, being self-employed, a business owner and an investor. You must become a business owner who invests. If you are not creating systems, you will not have time to invest or create that financial freedom that you truly desire. You are simply working your business like a job except you are taking all the risk with no long-term rewards. Systemize your business and analyze ways to create CASH Flow and intentionally use it to invest in real estate.

Automation

One of the challenges of being a small business owner is to manage every facet of your business. Often the owner oversees generating the sales and managing the process and closing the deals. Once this cycle is over you must start all over again. Unless you create an automation system that will allow you to juggle all the balls at once you will never begin to see the results you are looking for.

Step 3 Take time to Think and Grow Rich

Spend at least 30 minutes daily in deep thought. This is very important. This also means - No radio, TV, no computers, and no phone or emails. Shut out all the noise. Be sure that you have these 30 minutes daily. If you have a family let them know that you will need this time daily going forward. Do this in the morning or in the evening. It honestly does not matte when you do it if you do it. Many successful business people have a morning routine in which they either meditate, exercise or journal. If you can get up early enough in the morning, do it and make time for this. Creating this habit will be one of the best things you have ever done. Earl Nightingale recommends this in his book The Strangest Secret. So, this is not a new concept even it if is new for you. Give yourself time to Think and Grow Rich. Make a list of massive action steps that you will implement immediately for your business. Take the time to review what you have accomplished thus far and create the plan going forward on exactly how you will achieve more. You will be amazed at what you can create once you stop and Think and Grow Rich. Do this daily and even if some of your list has not been achieved, that is okay. The point is to continue generating ideas for your business from which you can take massive action.

Step 4 Systematize Your Why and Analyze the Ways

Your why is one of the most important aspects of your decision to operate a successful business long term. You must create systems for your business that will automate the work processes and allow you the time to analyze new ways to create Cash Flow that can be used to invest in other opportunities such as real estate. In Robert Kyosaki's Cash Flow Quadrant he talks about the roles of an employee, being self-employed, a business owner and an investor. It is important to embody all of these as he discusses so that you can gain all angles, to challenge yourself and get to level of an investor. You must become a business owner who invests. If you are not creating systems to help support you then you will not have time to invest. It is important to remember these quadrants when creating your strategy and systemizing your why. You do not want to be an employee or simply self-employed because in these areas you work for your money, but your money is not working for you. When you systemize your strategy you find a means to gain added passive income that allows money to flow without you actively working day in and day out to pursue this income The point is not to simply work your business like a job except because when you do that you are taking all of the risk with no long term rewards. Therefore, it is important that you set up the systems so that you can gain access to the rewards. Systemize your business and analyze ways to create CASH Flow and intentionally use it to invest in real estate.

Step 5 Create a Cash Flow Parking Lot or Product

Most small business owners start in business by leasing space from a landlord. If your business is located near a parking lot check for special permits that will allow you to create a Parking lot and charge fees. Or you can put in vending machines in an office building that you own to gain additional income. Or if you own an apartment building, you may be able to put in washers and dryers for a fee. There are many ways you can leverage your Cash Flow by being creative with what is available to you. This will allow you to create residual income to use to purchase the building, offset your lease payments or Invest in your own space. If the parking lot is not an option, create your own product.

The idea is to create ways to offset your expenses and create other streams of income that can be converted into additional CASHFLOW that can be used to invest in a long-term income strategy such as real estate.

Step 6: Get Your House in order by Getting Your Credit in Line

Most business owners who want to become investors start with the foundation of the house instead of developing a solid set of plans. Getting your house in order by getting your credit in line is the first step in establishing a solid foundation and building a house that will stand the test of time. Before you begin the process of creating cash flow, get a personal analysis on your personal finances to include an in depth look at your personal credit. Use your financial advisor to help you in understanding your personal financial foundation. Start by evaluating where you are so you can strategically move forward. Seek options for getting your scores in the 700 range. Once you can get your credit in line the doors will open, and you will be able to leverage your credit and begin to use it to get lines of credit that will allow you to take advantage of more opportunities to invest with CASH.

Step 7 Decide on the Ride

Decide on the investment vehicle you will use to create Cash Flow.

There are various ways to invest in real estate. Many start with residential and move into commercial properties. Decide on your Ride and take massive action to create the Cash Flow that can be used to create the financial freedom that will allow you to live to work instead of working to live.

RIDE- Residual Income Does Exist

It is more than just believing in yourself and your business. It is about taking strategic action to make your business work for you.

Your investment vehicle is your way to create Cash Flow, so you can live a financially free life and gain a greater return on your investment.

CONCLUSION

Cash Flow for Business Owners was not only designed for business owners, it was designed for any individual that have a desire to create residual income and change the trajectory of your family's financial future.

Personally, I believe that real estate is fastest and most reliable way to achieve those goals.

Use this book as a guide to help you formulate a plan and then take massive action. You will discover how fast and easy it is to achieve residual income through investing.

RESOURCES

The Cash Flow Coaching Program

I realized early on that it was my mission to help others do what I also wanted to do, and that is to become financially free. It can and will happen if you create a solid plan and follow the necessary action steps that ultimately create financial freedom.

If your desire is to achieve financial freedom and you simply don't know where to start, I have created a program that will assist you with achieving your goals.

The Cash Flow Coaching Program is designed to provide a solid plan of action for Business Owners to create residual Income by investing in real estate.

In this 90 Day Coaching Program you will walk away with the following:

1. Cash Flow for Business Owners- The Book

2. Cash Flow Plan for Real Estate Investors- Invest Ready for Existing Properties or New Construction

3. Cash Flow Plan for Real Estate Financing- Funding Your Dreams

4. Cash Flow Master Plan for Refinancing the Deal- Mortgage Ready

If you would like to get started today or want more information on any of our products or services, please email us at info.tunitabailey@gmail.com or visit our website at www.msbthemoneylady.com

Thank You

Tunita Bailey